Fast Ideas for Busy Teachers

Math

by
Anne Davies

Illustrations by
Kathryn Marlin

Published by Frank Schaffer Publications
an imprint of

 **Children's Publishing**

Author: Anne Davies
Editor: Cindy Barden

Children's Publishing

Published by Frank Schaffer Publications
An imprint of McGraw-Hill Children's Publishing
Copyright © 2004 McGraw-Hill Children's Publishing

Send all inquiries to:
McGraw-Hill Children's Publishing
3195 Wilson Drive NW
Grand Rapids, Michigan 49544

Fast Ideas for Busy Teachers: Math—Grade 3
ISBN: 0-7682-2913-8

1 2 3 4 5 6 7 8 9 MAL 09 08 07 06 05 04

The *McGraw·Hill* Companies

Table of Contents

0-7682-2913-8 *Fast Ideas for Busy Teachers: Math*

© McGraw-Hill Children's Publishing
0-7682-2913-8 *Fast Ideas for Busy Teachers: Math*

Introduction

Packed with hundreds of quick tips, fun ideas, and reproducibles, the *Fast Ideas for Busy Teachers: Math* series provides a wonderful resource designed to make a busy teacher's life easier. Ideas for stocking and organizing your math learning center, individual and group activities, games, reproducibles, patterns, puzzles, explorations of concepts, and much more invite students to learn about math through creative and fun hands-on activities.

Fast Ideas for Busy Teachers: Math supplements your math curriculum with warm-up or follow-up exercises, take-home pages, in-class assignments, and rainy-day activities to help students master a variety of mathematical concepts and skills. Organization by content related to various math skills makes it quick and easy to find the material you need, when you need it. A wide variety of open-ended material allows you to adapt activities to meet the specific needs of your class or individual students. Watch enthusiasm for math grow as students discover how valuable and fun learning math can be!

Teacher resource pages include organizational tips, suggestions for manipulatives, patterns, and a variety of individual, partner, and small group activities designed to increase students' understanding of math. Preparation time and supplies needed are minimal and include items normally available in classrooms.

Fast Ideas for Busy Teachers: Math topics and skill areas are based on the current NCTM Principles and Standards for School Mathematics, designed by the National Council of Teachers of Mathematics. They include number and operations; algebra; geometry; measurement; and data analysis and probability skills through problem-solving strategies, reasoning and proof, mathematical connections, representations, and communications. For specific information, see the matrix showing the correlation of the activities and tips to the NCTM Standards.

Fast Ideas for Busy Teachers: Math allows you to plan creative, motivating activities and incorporate them in your math curriculum. Best of all, students' enthusiasm for math grows when math becomes an adventure of fun and discovery!

0-7682-2913-8 *Fast Ideas for Busy Teachers: Math*

Meeting the NCTM Standards
Correlation Chart

	PROBLEM SOLVING	REASONING & PROOF	CONNECTIONS	REPRESENTATION	COMMUNICATION
NUMBER & OPERATIONS	7, 8, 9, 10, 11, 12, 13, 14, 15, 16, 17, 18, 22, 38, 39, 40, 41, 42, 43, 44, 45, 46, 47, 48, 50, 51, 52, 72, 73, 75, 76, 78	11, 35, 36, 38, 72, 73, 74, 75	8, 9, 10, 11, 12, 13, 14, 15, 16, 17, 19, 20, 21, 22, 26, 27, 28, 35, 36, 37, 38, 39, 40, 41, 42, 43, 44, 45, 46, 48, 50, 51, 52, 72, 74, 75, 77, 78	19, 20, 21, 22, 26, 27, 28, 29, 35, 36, 37, 44, 46, 47, 48, 49, 72, 73, 75, 77, 78	7, 8, 12, 15, 19, 20, 21, 22, 26, 35, 36, 37, 38, 42, 46, 47, 48, 49, 50, 77, 78
ALGEBRA	23, 24, 25	23, 24	23	23	23, 24
GEOMETRY	30, 34, 62	60, 61, 62	30, 33, 34, 60, 61, 62	30, 31, 32, 33, 34, 60, 61, 62	30, 31, 32, 33, 34, 60, 61, 62
MEASUREMENT	53, 54, 55, 57, 58, 67, 68, 69, 71	58, 67, 69, 70, 71	53, 54, 56, 57, 58, 67, 68, 69, 71	53, 54, 55, 58, 69, 71	53, 54, 57, 67, 69, 70, 71
DATA ANALYSIS & PROBABILITY	64, 65	63, 64, 65	63, 64, 65, 66	63, 64, 65, 66	63, 64, 66

0-7682-2913-8 *Fast Ideas for Busy Teachers: Math*

Addition and Subtraction

More

Students have fun reviewing addition and subtraction facts by playing variations of the classic card game "War."

For the addition version, the game can be called "More." To play, divide packs of playing cards or number cards equally among all players. Each player turns two cards faceup, adds them together, and compares the sum to the totals of the other players' cards. The player with the highest sum wins all of the cards, turns them over, and places them on the bottom of his or her pile.

In the event of a tie, players turn over one more card and add it to the sum. The player with the highest sum wins the round.

The game continues until one player collects all of the cards. For a more challenging game, players turn over three or four cards at a time, creating multi-step addition equations.

More or Less

To review subtraction facts, call the game "More or Less." Players turn over two cards and subtract the value of the lesser number from the value of the greater one. The player with the highest remainder takes all of the cards from that round of play.

Math Book Basket

Use a large wicker basket, laundry basket, or plastic tote to store featured math books in the math center. Replace the books in the basket periodically to include ones related to the current math unit. Students who complete in-class math assignments early can use their time to select and read a book from the math book basket.

Suggested Titles:

Jon Scieszka's humorous *Math Curse* invites readers to see math in the world all around them.

Any of the books in Stuart J. Murphy's *Math Start* series are great.

Denise Schmandt-Besserat's *The History of Counting* challenges students to think about a wide range of ways people have approached counting and representing numbers over the millennia.

Include folktales with a math twist like *A Grain of Rice* by Helena Clare Pittman.

0-7682-2913-8 *Fast Ideas for Busy Teachers: Math*

Addition and Subtraction

Mixed-Up Math Puzzles

With Mixed-Up Math Puzzles, you can offer students fun alternatives to humdrum drill-it worksheets to review their addition and subtraction facts. Cut the puzzles apart and give each student an envelope with the puzzle pieces. (Save one uncut copy for the answer key.) Students can work alone or in pairs to complete the puzzles.

Each puzzle includes 24 equations for students to solve. For addition and subtraction review of one- and two-digit numbers, make a copy of the activity "Mixed-Up Math Puzzle A" for each student.

For addition and subtraction review with three-digit numbers, students can complete the activity "Mixed-Up Math Puzzle B."

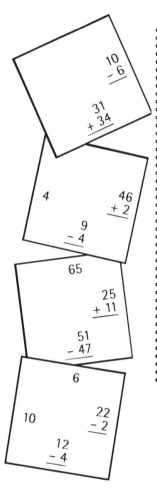

Create Your Own Math Puzzles

Create your own Mixed-Up Math Puzzles to review addition, subtraction, multiplication, or division facts using the template "Create Your Own Mixed-Up Math Puzzle."

Write the equations by the question marks and the corresponding answers in the blanks indicated by the arrows.

Challenge students to create their own Mixed-Up Math Puzzles using the template. This provides practice creating and solving equations. Have students check their answers using the inverse operation.

When they finish the puzzles, they can cut them apart and trade with a partner to solve.

0-7682-2913-8 *Fast Ideas for Busy Teachers: Math*

Mixed-Up Math Puzzle A ....

$\begin{array}{r} 10 \\ -\ 6 \\ \hline \end{array}$ $\begin{array}{r} 31 \\ +\ 34 \\ \hline \end{array}$	4 $\begin{array}{r} 46 \\ +\ 2 \\ \hline \end{array}$ $\begin{array}{r} 9 \\ -\ 4 \\ \hline \end{array}$	48 $\begin{array}{r} 14 \\ -\ 3 \\ \hline \end{array}$ $\begin{array}{r} 41 \\ +\ 5 \\ \hline \end{array}$	11 $\begin{array}{r} 8 \\ +\ 9 \\ \hline \end{array}$
65 $\begin{array}{r} 25 \\ +\ 11 \\ \hline \end{array}$ $\begin{array}{r} 51 \\ -\ 47 \\ \hline \end{array}$	5 36 $\begin{array}{r} 16 \\ +\ 3 \\ \hline \end{array}$ $\begin{array}{r} 12 \\ -\ 6 \\ \hline \end{array}$	46 $\begin{array}{r} 13 \\ +\ 18 \\ \hline \end{array}$ 19 $\begin{array}{r} 6 \\ +\ 6 \\ \hline \end{array}$	17 31 $\begin{array}{r} 9 \\ -\ 7 \\ \hline \end{array}$
4 $\begin{array}{r} 14 \\ -\ 4 \\ \hline \end{array}$ $\begin{array}{r} 9 \\ -\ 2 \\ \hline \end{array}$	6 10 $\begin{array}{r} 22 \\ -\ 2 \\ \hline \end{array}$ $\begin{array}{r} 12 \\ -\ 4 \\ \hline \end{array}$	12 $\begin{array}{r} 4 \\ +\ 11 \\ \hline \end{array}$ 20 $\begin{array}{r} 6 \\ +\ 8 \\ \hline \end{array}$	2 15 $\begin{array}{r} 7 \\ +\ 9 \\ \hline \end{array}$
7 $\begin{array}{r} 13 \\ +\ 5 \\ \hline \end{array}$	8 18 $\begin{array}{r} 5 \\ +\ 9 \\ \hline \end{array}$	14 $\begin{array}{r} 10 \\ +\ 12 \\ \hline \end{array}$ 14	16 22

0-7682-2913-8 *Fast Ideas for Busy Teachers: Math*

Mixed-Up Math Puzzle B ....

345 + 276 198 + 324	621 783 − 276 903 − 464	165 507 + 148 245 − 119	313 712 − 258
522 363 + 217 643 − 246	439 694 580 + 245 321 − 270	126 742 939 − 163 68 + 43	454 579 318 + 21
397 521 − 145 120 + 98	51 254 376 + 578 832 + 377	111 845 832 − 627 1,654 − 986	339 218 472 + 298
218 525 − 327	1,209 458 198 + 562	668 158 1,020 − 39	770 119

© McGraw-Hill Children's Publishing   0-7682-2913-8 *Fast Ideas for Busy Teachers: Math*

Create Your Own Mixed-Up Math Puzzle ....

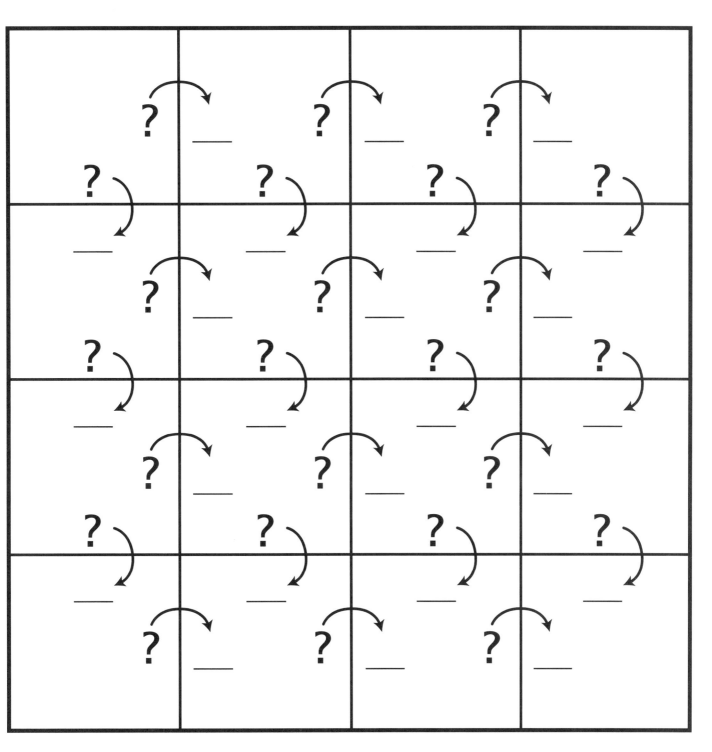

0-7682-2913-8 *Fast Ideas for Busy Teachers: Math*

Addition and Subtraction and Rounding Whole Numbers

Thumbs Up, Thumbs Down

Review rounding numbers with this quick practice activity. Write a number on the board and ask students to indicate if it should be rounded up or down with a show of thumbs—thumbs up if the number should be rounded up and thumbs down if it should be rounded down.

Mr. Top's Trophy Shop

Ask students, "What do you think would happen if we got rid of all pennies, nickels, quarters, and dimes?"

Like Mr. Top of Mr. Top's Trophy Shop, they may be tired of figuring out change for people. However, if he got rid of coins, Mr. Top would need to adjust prices.

Give each student a copy of the activity, "Mr. Top's Trophy Shop." Tell them Mr. Top has decided he is tired of counting out pennies, nickels, quarters, and dimes, and making change. Students need to go through the store and round all the prices to the nearest dollar so he'll never, ever have to make change with coins again.

Addition and Subtraction Places, Please

Shortly before they line up for recess, lunch, or dismissal, divide students into small groups. Give each group an index card with a different addition or subtraction equation to solve. (Make the equations more difficult than usual, but solvable.) Students work together to solve the equations and double-check the answers. They write the answer on the backs of the cards.

When all groups finish, have them line up in order based on the answers to the equations, with the group who had the greater (or least) answer going first.

Sam's Ice Cream Shop

Give each student a copy of the activity "Sam's Ice Cream Shop." Tell them Sam's Ice Cream Shop is located in a very unusual town. All the citizens of this town have agreed to eliminate pennies, nickels, and quarters. They simply don't want to bother with them anymore, but they will keep dimes.

Sam, the owner of Sam's Ice Cream Shop, needs their help changing the prices on all of his ice cream treats, rounding them to the nearest dime.

0-7682-2913-8 *Fast Ideas for Busy Teachers: Math*

Name _____ Date _____

 # Mr. Top's Trophy Shop ....

Engraving 70¢ per line
New Price: _____

Assorted Ribbons 3 for $1.18
New Price: _____

Regular Rabbit Trophy $5.95
New Price: _____

Best in Show Rabbit Trophy $10.82
New Price: _____

Best in Show Dog Trophy $12.25
New Price: _____

Regular Dog Trophy $6.30
New Price: _____

Swimming Trophy $7.45
New Price: _____

Basketball MVP Award $11.65
New Price: _____

Soccer Cup $27.99
New Price: _____

Soccer MVP Award $11.55
New Price: _____

13

Sam's Ice Cream Shop ....

Round the prices to the nearest dime. Write the new prices.

Milk Shakes

Small: $1.82

New Price: _____

Medium: $2.77

New Price: _____

Large: $3.69

New Price: _____

Sundaes

Small: $1.99

New Price: _____

Medium: $2.86

New Price: _____

Large: $4.06

New Price: _____

Cones

Single Dip: $1.10

New Price: _____

Double Dip: $2.07

New Price: _____

Triple Dip: $3.04

New Price: _____

Extras

Nuts: 25¢

New Price: _____

Whipped Cream: 44¢

New Price: _____

Sprinkles: 33¢

New Price: _____

0-7682-2913-8 *Fast Ideas for Busy Teachers: Math*

Keep the Balloon in the Air

Challenging students to see how long they can keep a balloon in the air can be a fun way to encourage teamwork while practicing skip counting skills. Have students count each time the balloon is tapped as they work together to keep it in the air, but instead of counting by 1s, the person who taps the balloons counts by 2s, 3s, 4s, 5s, or 10s (designate in advance).

If your students need support with skip counting, post a 100 number board with the appropriate skip counting numbers marked. To make the activity more challenging, have students begin skip counting at 37, 65, or anywhere else between 1 and 100!

A-Mazing Fours

The activity, "A-Mazing Fours" provides a fun way to skip count by 4s. Before giving students a copy of the maze, draw the mini-maze example shown below on the board. Explain that the idea is to complete the maze by drawing a line over the numbers that skip count by 4s. Practice together on the mini-maze.

How Many Cans? Skip Counting by 5s

The nickel deposit on cans provides a great way to link skip counting to real world math. Challenge students to use skip counting to figure out how many cans someone would need to return in order to buy these items: an ice cream cone that costs 95¢; a 75¢ sports card at a yard sale; a 50¢ pack of gum; an 80¢ ride on a bus, etc.

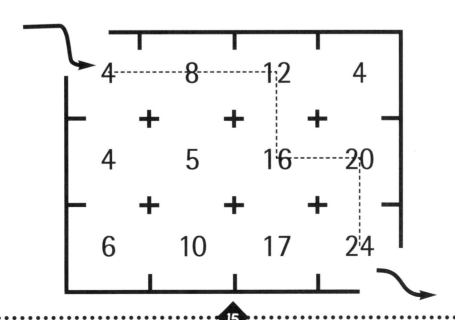

    0-7682-2913-8 *Fast Ideas for Busy Teachers: Math*

A-Mazing Fours...

Draw a line to find your way through this maze. Follow the numbers that skip count by four.

Start →

4	8	12	16	18	20	24
+	+	+	+	+	+	
8	16	18	20	25	34	49
+	+	+	+	+	+	
10	2	14	24	80	84	42
+	+	+	+	+	+	
34	54	32	28	32	36	40
+	+	+	+	+	+	
50	12	36	16	22	31	90
+	+	+	+	+	+	
48	44	40	24	62	72	94
+	+	+	+	+	+	
52	3	12	49	5	24	10
+	+	+	+	+	+	
56	40	39	76	80	84	88
+	+	+	+	+	+	
60	64	68	72	21	7	92
+	+	+	+	+	+	
68	34	38	74	78	84	96

→ 100

0-7682-2913-8 *Fast Ideas for Busy Teachers: Math*

Skip Counting to 100

Skip Counting Sequence Search

For additional skip counting practice, students can complete the activity "Skip Counting Sequence Search." The grid includes skip counting sequences by 2s, 3s, 4s, 5s, and 10s.

You can adjust this activity to match students' abilities. If students have had little practice skip counting, ask them to look only for specific patterns, such as skip counting by 2s and 10s.

You could reuse this activity later in the year and have students search for the other sequences. A few students may even discover the two skip counting by 20s sequences.

On Your Mark, Get Set, Go!

One way for students to practice skip counting, particularly by 2s, 5s, or 10s, is to race against a calculator and see who can skip count faster—people or machines. This could be a whole group activity with all members of the class racing against one person with a calculator or one-on-one with students working in pairs.

To make it fair, the student using the calculator must press the plus sign, the number, and the equal sign each time. If skip counting by 2s, the student using the calculator would press 2, then + 2 =, then + 2 =, over and over to 100, while students without calculators simply say the numbers to skip count to 100.

May the best skip counter win!

The Grapes of Math Read Aloud

Reading the riddles and discussing the pictures and problems in Greg Tang's *The Grapes of Math* and *Math Appeal: Mind-Stretching Math Riddles* as a group are great ways to practice skip counting skills and to recognize how skip counting can help solve math stories.

Be certain everyone can see the pictures as you read. After reading a riddle, ask students, "Can skip counting help us here? How?"

Sometimes the answer is straightforward as in the first spread of either of these books where they simply skip count by 4s or 5s to find the answers. At other times, students will need to add first, then skip count (as in the "Grapes of Math" riddle) or skip count and then add or subtract (as in the "Snail Parade" riddle). This provides multi-step problem-solving practice. After they've found a solution, ask students to write a math sentence for the equation.

0-7682-2913-8 *Fast Ideas for Busy Teachers: Math*

Skip Counting Sequence Search ....

Look left, right, up, down, and diagonally to find the skip counting sequences hidden in this number grid. Circle the skip counting sequences with at least three numbers in a row.

99	77	98	88	78	68	58
88	96	86	76	20	24	46
94	84	93	25	30	43	65
82	90	30	90	40	55	100
87	35	55	75	50	90	66
40	12	62	45	80	64	18
44	42	40	70	62	85	58
22	35	44	60	56	55	90
30	46	58	46	52	72	92
39	56	36	100	48	57	60
54	36	96	43	44	50	62
26	92	33	38	40	42	52
88	23	28	30	32	34	36
13	18	23	28	27	31	35

0-7682-2913-8 *Fast Ideas for Busy Teachers: Math*

Collecting and Organizing Data

What We Learned About Us

This activity can be particularly interesting if used at the beginning of the school year when you and the students are still getting to know each other.

Creating a class book of data about the group introduces students to data collecting and graphing while building class unity. Ask students to brainstorm for questions to ask and types of data they could collect to use to make graphs.

Some suggestions:

- How many boys and girls are in the class?
- How many classmates have sisters?
- How many have brothers?
- What is your favorite movie?
- Which sport do you like best?
- Who is your favorite author?

Students can choose a question to answer and work in pairs to collect data and organize it into some form of graph. Each pair should create at least one page for the class book. If possible, have students include a variety of different types of graphs including picture graphs, pie charts, bar graphs, line graphs, and Venn diagrams. Each pair of students can present their findings to the class and share the graphs they made. You can combine graphs in a three-ring binder to keep in the math center.

Getting Into the Graph

One way to help students understand graphing is to have them physically become part of the graph. Begin with a simple yes or no question (Do you like spinach?) Have students form two lines, one for yes and one for no. Students in each line can count off. Write the totals for each group on the board, and have students convert the information into a simple graph.

Variations:

Ask students to choose between two or three options (Do you like chocolate, vanilla, or mint ice cream best?) and have them line up according to their responses.

Take a Vote

Use any occasion when students vote to model different techniques for collecting and presenting data. Voting by a show of hands is a quick, easy method. Also consider other methods such as having students use chips to drop in ballot boxes (this works well if you have a yes or no question,) or by filling in secret ballots. Involve students in counting votes and deciding how to present the results.

To support an exploration of voting data, read Stuart J. Murphy's *The Grizzly Gazette* in which a group of summer campers takes opinion polls and makes numerous pie charts in the camp mascot election.

© McGraw-Hill Children's Publishing   0-7682-2913-8 *Fast Ideas for Busy Teachers: Math*

Collecting and Organizing Data

Breaking News

Students see poll results in newspapers and hear them on television. Many Internet sites ask people to vote on a "question of the day." This activity encourages students to think through the data in several different ways and to connect their ways of organizing data with methods used by others.

Using "The Breaking News Press" template, students can report on the results of a weekly question in a "real world" newspaper format. The template includes space for a headline, the question asked, a visual representation of the results in the form of a graph, and a brief "article" on the findings. (Remind students to answer who, what, when, where, why, and how in the article.)

You could assign two students as reporters each week to work together at completing the survey and preparing the final report. Post a copy of the finished "newspaper" on a bulletin board and make copies for students to take home and share with their families.

A Tiger for a Teacher

Tiger Math: Learning to Graph from a Baby Tiger by Ann Whitehead Nagda and Cindy Bickel offers a meaningful, highly intriguing introduction to graphing. Who can resist photographs of a cuddly baby tiger? Most students will also enjoy watching the baby grow and develop. Within this compelling context, Nagda and Bickel introduce picture graphs, pie charts, bar graphs, and line graphs. Reading this book with your class is a perfect introduction to these important ways of organizing data.

Who Lives on the Busiest Street?

For experience gathering data through observation instead of interviews, ask students to spend 10 minutes observing and taking notes on who and what passes by in front of their homes. Using the observation sheet, "How Busy Is My Street?" students keep a tally of events, total up their tallies, and make simple line graphs showing their results. (Demonstrate or review how to use tally marks if necessary.)

Post the completed surveys and pose the questions:

Who lives on the busiest street?

How do we know that?

Opinions may vary. Do more cars or more people make a street busy? Students may realize that having data doesn't always mean having answers.

0-7682-2913-8 *Fast Ideas for Busy Teachers: Math*

The Breaking News Press ....

Survey Says

_____

_____

Our Question	Our Results

In a recent poll taken by reporters _____ and _____,

we discovered _____

_____

_____

_____

_____

0-7682-2913-8 *Fast Ideas for Busy Teachers: Math*

How Busy Is My Street?................................

I gathered my data starting at _____:_____ and ending at _____:_____.

My tallies:

People walking	Cars	Trucks	Bicycles

My Totals:

I counted _____ people walking past my house.

I counted _____ cars driving past my house.

I counted _____ trucks driving past my house.

I counted _____ people riding bicycles past my house.

Complete the graph. Make an X for each car, truck, bike rider, or person walking that you saw.

 My Graph

people walking
cars
trucks
people riding bikes

0-7682-2913-8 *Fast Ideas for Busy Teachers: Math*

Finding the Value of Variables

How Many in My Hand?

Students work together in this simple game using manipulatives to find variables in equations.

Divide students into pairs. Give each student a handful of small manipulatives and a copy of the activity page "Numbers and Equations We Explored." The manipulatives should be small enough that a student can hold up to 15 or so in one hand with the hand closed. (Pennies, small game chips, or bread tags work well.)

To play, one student closes his or her eyes while the other student chooses a number, counts out that many manipulatives, hides some of the manipulatives in his hand, and leaves the rest on the desk. The student holding the manipulatives invites his or her partner to open his eyes and says, "There are 3 pennies on the table and 10 pennies altogether. How many are in my hand?"

When the partner correctly answers the question, they switch roles and continue.

Students can record the results on the activity page. This also provides practice writing math sentences.

Where Did I Begin?

Students can work in pairs to play "Where Did I Begin?" It is another game to practice finding variables. Ask one student in each pair to think of a number between 1 and 100, but not say the number. Tell them to do something to that number, such as adding 10 or subtracting 3. Encourage mental math, but allow paper and pencil for students who need them.

Students tell their partners their new number and ask, "Where did I begin?" Again, encourage students to use mental math to find the answers.

You may want to play a few rounds as a class until students become familiar with the game.

If students are ready for the challenge, give them two directions after they have chosen their numbers (Example: add two, then subtract four).

What's Missing? Cross Number Puzzles

Most students are familiar with crossword puzzles, but number puzzles may be new. Explain that instead of writing words, the answers are numerals. After students finish the "Cross Number Puzzle" activity page, challenge them to create their own cross number puzzles. Add these to the math center to use another day.

0-7682-2913-8 *Fast Ideas for Busy Teachers: Math*

Name _____ Date _____

Finding the Value of Variables

 # Numbers and Equations We Explored.....

1. Number chosen: _____

   We (added   subtracted) _____ from that number.

   The new number was _____.

   Write the math sentence: _____

2. Number chosen: _____

   We (added   subtracted) _____ from that number.

   The new number was _____.

   Write the math sentence: _____

3. Number chosen: _____

   We (added   subtracted) _____ from that number.

   The new number was _____.

   Write the math sentence: _____

4. Number chosen: _____

   We (added   subtracted) _____ from that number.

   The new number was _____.

   Write the math sentence: _____

5. Number chosen: _____

   We (added   subtracted) _____ from that number.

   The new number was _____.

   Write the math sentence: _____

0-7682-2913-8 *Fast Ideas for Busy Teachers: Math*

Name _____ Date _____

What's Missing?
A Cross Number Puzzle..................................

Fill in the missing numerals to make the number sentences true.

40 − ___ = 18

−

51 − ___ = 42

=   −

33 − ___ = 9   ___ + 17 = 34

+   =   7

___ − 12 = 25

=

51 − ___ = 44

−

___ − 8 = 8

=

40 − ___ = 28

−

19

© McGraw-Hill Children's Publishing

0-7682-2913-8 *Fast Ideas for Busy Teachers: Math*

Reading and Writing Whole Numbers to 100,000

Check the Checks

Having students explore check writing and double-check the amounts is a great way to practice reading large whole numbers.

Show students a blank check or draw one on the board. Go through each item on the check and explain its purpose. Tell students that the amounts are written in both words and numbers so banks can double-check the amount before cashing it. Also point out that people often write what the check is for on the line along the bottom of the check.

After students complete the two-page activity "Check the Checks," ask various students to explain their reasons for accepting or rejecting each check.

"Magic" Money

After students have practiced checking checks for the West Bank of the Mississippi, ask them to imagine what they would do if they were given $500,000 in a Magic Money checking account. The tricky thing about "Magic" Money is that they only get three checks and must give away or spend all of the money in the account by writing three separate checks. Have students cut pieces of construction paper to represent their three checks and fill them in using the format and examples on the "Check the Checks" activity pages.

Remind students to write who the check is from, who it is to, the amount of the check in both standard notation and in words, and what the check is for. This helps you confirm that students are able to write large numbers in both standard notation and word form.

How Many Numbers Can You Make?

If you have a few extra minutes at the end of a class, students can practice reading and writing large whole numbers. Write five digits on the board in a column. Ask the questions listed and have students write the answers. Reading their answers gives students practice reading large numbers aloud.

What is the largest number you can make with these digits?

What is the smallest number you can make using all the digits?

How many different numbers can you make with these numbers?

0-7682-2913-8 *Fast Ideas for Busy Teachers: Math*

Name _____ Date _____

 # Check the Checks—Part 1......................

At your job at the West Bank of the Mississippi, you often cash checks for customers. Before you give anyone money, you must make sure there are no mistakes.

Check the checks to be certain the numerals and number words on the checks match exactly. If a check is correct, circle the word "Accept." If it is wrong, circle the word "Reject."

Mr. Top's Trophy Shop   101
1136 Kirkwood Court   Date _____ 9/27/04 _____
Hannibal, MO

Pay to the order of _____ Samuel Clemens Trophy Company _____ | $ 24,808 | **ACCEPT**

_____ Twenty-four thousand, eighty-eight _____ Dollars   **REJECT**

West Bank of the Mississippi
Hannibal, MO

For _____ trophies _____   Signed _____ S. Top _____

Mr. Top's Trophy Shop   102
1136 Kirkwood Court   Date _____ 9/27/04 _____
Hannibal, MO

Pay to the order of _____ Tom Sawyer _____ | $ 1,084 | **ACCEPT**

_____ One thousand and eighty-four _____ Dollars   **REJECT**

West Bank of the Mississippi
Hannibal, MO

For _____ Fence painting _____   Signed _____ S. Top _____

0-7682-2913-8 *Fast Ideas for Busy Teachers: Math*

Name _____ Date _____

 # Check the Checks—Part 2 ....

Mr. Top's Trophy Shop   103
1136 Kirkwood Court   Date _____ 9/27/04 _____
Hannibal, MO

Pay to the order of _____ Becky Thatcher's Trophy Company _____ | $ 10,840 | **ACCEPT**

_____ Ten thousand, eight hundred and four _____ Dollars   **REJECT**

West Bank of the Mississippi
Hannibal, MO

For ____ engraving machine ____   Signed _____ S. Top _____

Mr. Top's Trophy Shop   104
1136 Kirkwood Court   Date _____ 9/27/04 _____
Hannibal, MO

Pay to the order of _____ Mark Twain _____ | $ 11,145 | **ACCEPT**

_____ Eleven hundred and forty-five _____ Dollars   **REJECT**

West Bank of the Mississippi
Hannibal, MO

For ____ October rent ____   Signed _____ S. Top _____

Mr. Top's Trophy Shop   105
1136 Kirkwood Court   Date _____ 9/27/04 _____
Hannibal, MO

Pay to the order of _____ Huck Finn's Office Supply Company _____ | $ 1,202 | **ACCEPT**

_____ One thousand, two hundred and two _____ Dollars   **REJECT**

West Bank of the Mississippi
Hannibal, MO

For ____ computer repairs ____   Signed _____ S. Top _____

     0-7682-2913-8 *Fast Ideas for Busy Teachers: Math*

Name _____ Date _____

 # Hidden Numbers ....

Find and circle the numbers listed in the clues below.

Hint: It may help to write the number in standard form below the clue before you look for it.

Sixty-one thousand, seventy-two

(_____)

Thirteen thousand, four hundred sixty-eight

(_____)

Twenty-two thousand, six hundred seventeen

(_____)

Fifty thousand, seven hundred twenty-one

(_____)

Seventy-eight thousand, twenty-four

(_____)

100,000 + 400 + 20 + 4

(_____)

2,000 + 200 + 1

(_____)

80,000 + 8,000 + 600 + 1

(_____)

14,000 + 200 + 2

(_____)

17,000 + 900 + 20

(_____)

18,000 + 10 + 2

(_____)

45,000 + 1

(_____)

```
9 6 7 8 0 2 4 5 9
1 3 4 6 8 1 3 3 5
0 4 0 1 8 0 1 2 0
0 2 9 1 6 8 9 1 7
4 2 0 2 0 5 3 5 2
2 6 4 6 1 0 7 2 1
4 1 4 2 0 2 0 2 6
1 7 9 2 0 4 0 0 2
8 1 6 4 5 0 0 1 3
```

0-7682-2913-8 *Fast Ideas for Busy Teachers: Math*

Describing and Comparing Two- and Three-Dimensional Shapes

Geometric Shape Concentration

Concentration helps students focus on the attributes of different shapes. Copy the two pages of "Geometric Shapes Concentration Cards" onto cardstock, (laminate, if possible) and cut apart to make a sturdy set of reusable concentration cards with two- and three-dimensional shapes.

Game Option 1: When students turn over two cards that match, they must name the shape to keep the cards.

Game Option 2: For an additional challenge, have players name one fact about the shape for each pair they collect. (For example, if a student turns up a pair of triangles, he could say, "A triangle has three sides.")

Twenty Questions

Playing "Twenty Questions" can be a great way to review the attributes of two- and three-dimensional geometric shapes. Use one each of the geometric shape concentration cards. The first player selects a card, looks at the shape, but doesn't tell anyone what it is.

Classmates can ask up to twenty yes or no questions to try to figure out the shape on the card the player drew. This helps students become familiar with terms that describe geometric shapes.

Geometric Properties Line-Up

For a quick review of the properties of different shapes, give each row or table group one of the geometric shape concentration cards. Invite the group whose shape has specific properties (four right angles, three straight sides, six congruent faces, etc.) to line up first for lunch, recess, or dismissal.

Overnight Game Check-out

Encourage additional math practice and family involvement by allowing students to "check out" math games overnight from the math center.

Overnight game checkout could be an option for those interested. You could also give students a list of games they could check out and play at home in place of regular homework.

Zipper sandwich bags or small plastic containers containing the game pieces with stickers identifying the games make this option easier to manage. When students take games home, there's some risk that pieces may be lost, but the additional practice may be worth it.

0-7682-2913-8 *Fast Ideas for Busy Teachers: Mat*

Geometric Shapes Concentration Cards......

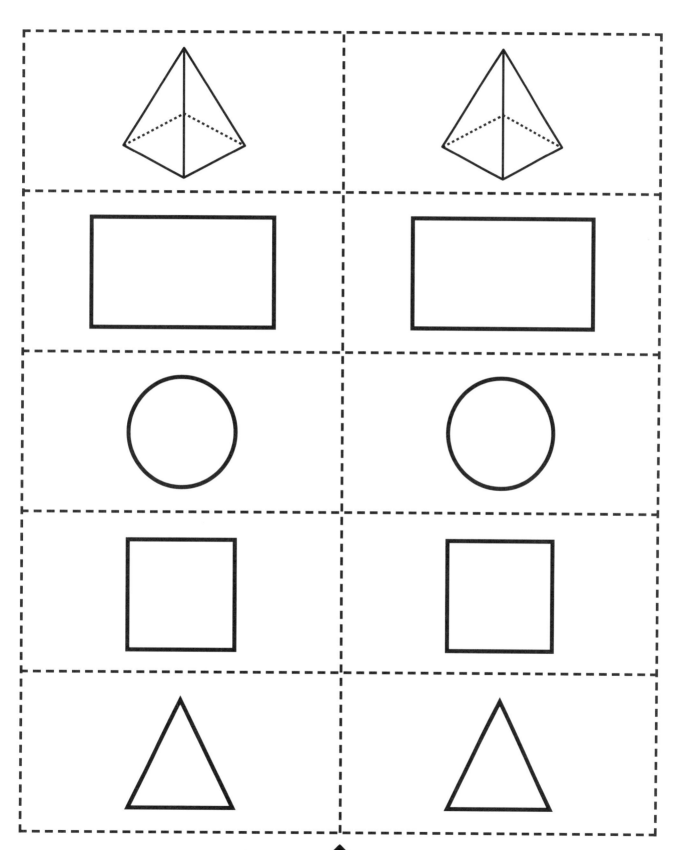

McGraw-Hill Children's Publishing

0-7682-2913-8 *Fast Ideas for Busy Teachers: Math*

Geometric Shapes Concentration Cards....

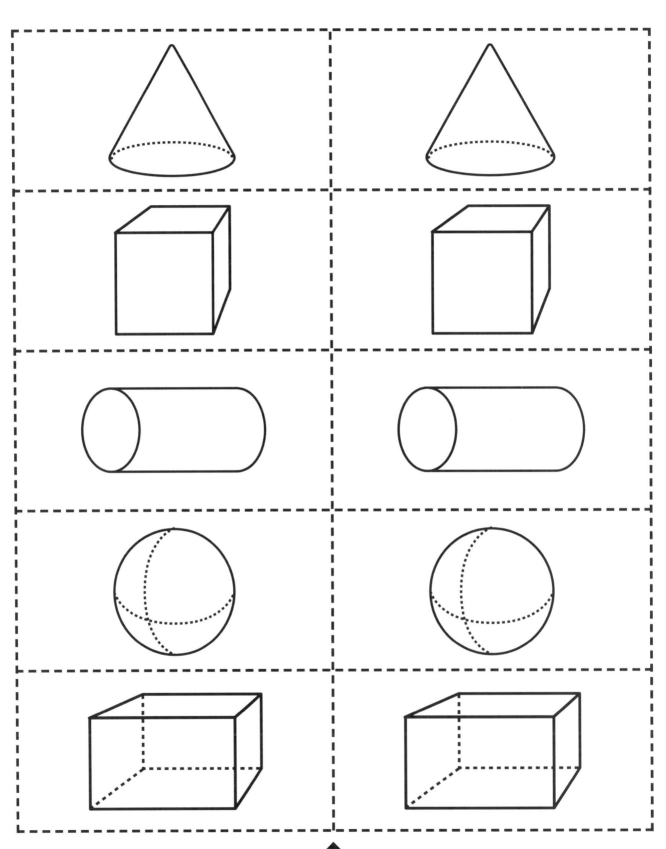

0-7682-2913-8 *Fast Ideas for Busy Teachers: Math*

Describing and Comparing Two- and Three-Dimensional Shapes

Shape Hunt

Encourage students to connect what they learn about shapes with their daily lives by playing "Shape Hunt." For this game, cut photos from magazines or use pages from a picture book. Divide students into teams. Show all students a picture and ask one person from each team to list all the geometric shapes their team can find in the picture in two or three minutes.

Go through the teams' lists together. Teams score one point for each shape they found. Teams score two points for a shape if no other team found that shape in the picture.

Math Book Basket

David Adler's *Shape Up! Fun with Triangles and other Polygons* is a great book to keep in the math book basket while students are working on geometric shapes. The book provides an engaging introduction to two-dimensional shapes from triangles to dodecagons.

What's in the Box?

This three-person game helps students identify, visualize, and describe three-dimensional shapes. To play, you will need a shoe box with a hole cut in one end large enough for a child's hand and three-dimensional models of a cube, a sphere, a rectangular prism, a cylinder, and a square pyramid.

You can use a Ping-Pong™ ball or similar-sized ball for the sphere. For the cylinder, use the cardboard tube from a toilet paper roll with two cardstock circles cut and taped to cover the ends. If you need manipulatives for the other shapes, copy the templates for "What's in the Box?" onto cardstock, then cut, fold, and tape as indicated.

To play, the first player selects a shape to put in the shoe box for the first round of the game. The other two players should not see what that shape is. The second player puts a hand in the shoe box to feel the shape and describes the shape without using its name. The third player uses the description given to name the shape. Students take turns being first, second, and third until they have named all the shapes.

On another occasion, give students a copy of the page of shapes for "What's in the Box?" to take home and make as a homework assignment.

0-7682-2913-8 *Fast Ideas for Busy Teachers: Math*

What's in the Box? Patterns ....

Cut along the solid lines.
Fold along the dotted lines.
Tape the edges of each figure together.

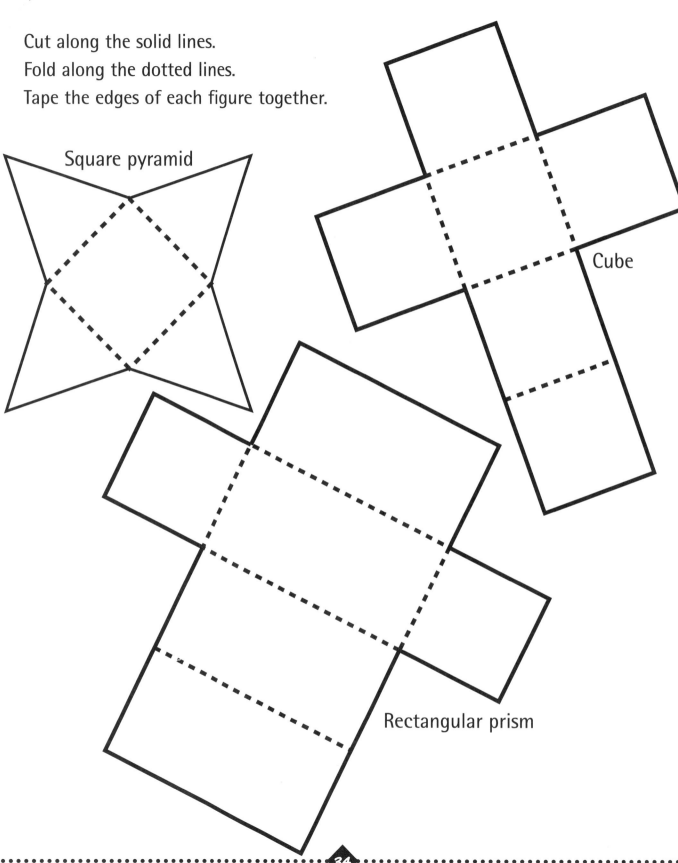

Square pyramid

Cube

Rectangular prism

0-7682-2913-8 *Fast Ideas for Busy Teachers: Math*

Representing, Comparing, and Ordering Large Numbers

We Have . . ./Who Has . . .?

The math game "We Have . . ./Who Has . . .?" helps students become familiar with large numbers. Make a copy of the "We Have . . ./Who Has . . .?" game cards, cut them apart, and mix them up. Divide students into pairs. Give each pair one card. All cards should be used so the answers will make a full circle back to the pair of students who began the game.

Ask one pair to begin by reading the "Who Has . . .?" portion of their card. Classmates should check the "We Have . . ." portion of their cards to see if they have the matching answer.

The pair with the matching card answers "We Have . . ." then reads their "Who Has . . .?" question. The game continues until the two students who started the game respond, "We have . . . ." Collect cards and redistribute them for another round.

> ### Oddball Number Puzzle Cards
>
> Save students' Oddball Number Puzzle cards in the math center to use as puzzles for the class to explore another day, for a rainy-day activity, or for students who complete their work early.

Oddball Number Puzzle

"Oddball Number Puzzles" challenge students to use several ways to represent a number. To introduce the game, write a large number on the board. Ask students to think about other ways to represent this number. Some students will think of expanded notation; others may think of a variety of equations.

Write all their suggestions on the board. Then add a number or equation that is incorrect—an oddball number. Ask students, "Does this number belong?"

Once they see why it does not belong, tell them you added it so there will be an oddball number (or equation). Explain that finding the oddball number would be a good math puzzle for someone who hadn't helped make up the collection of numbers on the board. Repeat with other numbers to be certain students understand.

Have students create their own oddball puzzles. Ask each student to write a collection of ways to represent a number on one side of an index card, along with one (and only one) oddball number or equation. On the back of the card, they should write only the oddball number/equation.

0-7682-2913-8 *Fast Ideas for Busy Teachers: Math*

We Have . . ./Who Has . . .? Game Cards

We have 1,000 + 100 + 20 + 1 Who has 20,342?	We have 20,000 + 300 + 40 + 2 Who has 16,789? 
We have 16,000 + 700 + 80 + 9 Who has 6,554?	We have 6,000 + 500 + 50 + 4 Who has 100,002? 
We have 100,000 + 2 Who has 35,967?	We have 35,000 + 900 + 60 + 7 Who has 99,222? 
We have 99,000 + 200 + 20 + 2 Who has 60,890?	We have 60,000 + 800 + 90 Who has 99, 244?
We have 99,000 + 200 + 40 + 4 Who has 12?	We have 10 + 2 Who has 7,456? 
We have 7,000 + 400 + 50 + 6 Who has 55,674?	We have 55,000 + 600 + 70 + 4 Who has 985? 
We have 900 + 80 + 5 Who has 6,894?	We have 6,000 + 800 + 90 + 4 Who has 1,678? 
We have 1,000 + 600 + 70 + 8 Who has 45,005?	We have 45,000 + 5 Who has 1,121? 

36

Representing, Comparing, and Ordering Large Numbers

Large Number Line-Up

Write large numbers on index cards, one number per card. Make one card for each student.

Distribute cards and tell students they are going to put the numbers on all the cards in order, by putting themselves in the same order.

Ask one student to stand in front of the class and name the number on her card. Call on a second student to read his number. Ask that student "Is your number greater or less than the first one?"

If his number is less, he lines up in front of the first student. If greater, he lines up behind her.

Continue calling on students and having them place themselves in front of, behind, or between students already standing, based on the numbers on their cards.

Once students are lined up, ask them to read their numbers in order from least to greatest.

Large Number Search

When you have a few extra minutes at the end of a class, challenge students to open any of their textbooks other than math and search for the largest number they can find in a given amount of time (two or three minutes). Have students write the numbers on the board, then compare and find the greatest number.

In addition to practice comparing large numbers, this activity provides an opportunity for students to think about how large numbers are used in other contexts besides math.

More Great Titles for Your Math Book Basket

Large numbers can be difficult for children and adults to conceptualize, but David M. Schwartz's *How Much Is a Million?* makes use of children's heights, goldfish, the time it takes to count, and drawings of tiny little stars to make a million, a billion, and a trillion much more imaginable.

Big Numbers and Pictures That Show Just How Big They Are by Edward Packard has a similar mission.

For those who don't want to stop at a trillion there's *On Beyond a Million: An Amazing Math Journey* by David M. Schwartz, which uses exponential counting to take readers to the googol and googolplex.

0-7682-2913-8 *Fast Ideas for Busy Teachers: Math*

Solving Multi-Step Math Stories

How Many Steps Forward?

Help students practice solving multi-step math stories by playing "How Many Steps Forward?" It is a simple board game in which a player advances farther on a given turn by solving a more complex math story.

Make a copy of the game cards and board on cardstock for each group. Cut the game cards apart. Players can use paper clips, play coins, game chips, etc., for game markers. They will also need scrap paper and pencils.

Players take turns selecting a game card. If a player solves a one-step story, he advances one space on the game board. If she solves a two-step story, she advances two spaces, and so on. If the player does not solve the math story correctly, play passes to the next player, who tries to solve it. The number of spaces a player moves is shown on the cards in parentheses.

Solutions can be found in the Answer Key at the end of the book.

You can make additional cards for the game by writing your own math stories or using some from any math book. Be sure to include the number of spaces to be moved in parentheses on each card.

Easy Math, Tricky Words

To solve multi-step math stories, paying close attention to the words in the math stories is important. To help students understand how important it is to read carefully, read *Easy Math Puzzles* by David Adler aloud to your class. The math stories challenge students to think about the context in which math is used.

Option:

Use some of the puzzles from the book as warm-ups or special math challenges.

Arithme-Tickle: Riddle-Rhymes to Make Problem-Solving Fun

Some students are quick to say, "I don't get it" or "I'm stuck" when faced with a multiple-step math story. Reading one or two riddles a day from J. Patrick Lewis's *Arithme-Tickle: An Even Number of Odd Riddle-Rhymes* aloud to the class can help these reluctant mathematicians see how stories can be broken down into steps and solved. The 18 riddles, most using addition and subtraction, require students to think through a series of steps to find an answer. Students can work in pairs or small groups to solve a riddle after you read it aloud and share the picture.

When you finish reading the book to the class, be sure to add *Arithme-Tickle* to the math book basket or learning center so students can continue to explore and review it.

 0-7682-2913-8 *Fast Ideas for Busy Teachers: Math*

How Many Steps Forward? Game Board

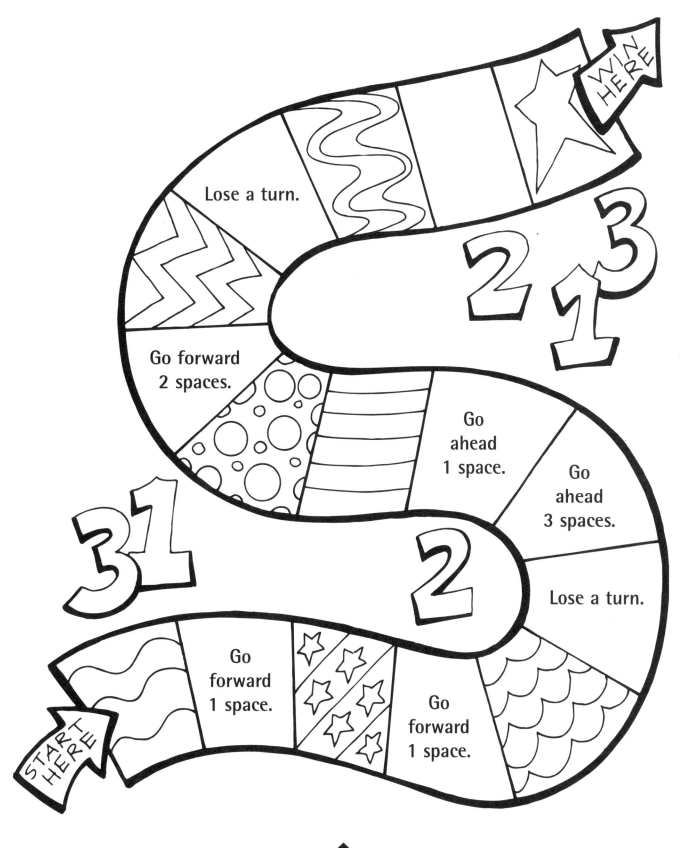

0-7682-2913-8 *Fast Ideas for Busy Teachers: Math*

How Many Steps Forward? Game Cards

1

Lincoln School has 350 students. There are 38 teachers and teachers' aides. They all eat school lunches. How many lunches must the kitchen make? (1)

5

Longfellow School has 245 students. On Monday, they had a choice of turkey or macaroni and cheese for lunch. 29 students chose turkey. 78 students brought their own lunch. How many chose macaroni and cheese? (2)

2

Jackson School has 452 students. They have 49 teachers and teachers' aides. 23 of the teachers bring their own lunches. Everyone else eats school lunches. How many lunches must the kitchen make? (2)

6

Sam got on an elevator with two other people. On the second floor, one person got off and two got on. On the fourth floor, two people got off and no one got on. On the sixth floor, three people and a poodle got on. How many people were in the elevator then? (3)

3

Wilson School has 338 students. There are 35 teachers and teachers' aides. 23 of the teachers bring their own lunches. 97 of the students bring their own lunches. Everyone else eats school lunches. How many lunches must the kitchen make? (3)

7

Carmen baked 456 cookies on Tuesday and sold 377. On Wednesday, she baked 200 more and sold 220. How many did she have left when she closed her bakery Wednesday night? (3)

4

Roosevelt School has 333 students. On Friday, students had a choice of fish sandwiches or cheeseburgers for lunch. 92 students chose fish sandwiches. How many chose cheeseburgers? (1)

8

The Cupcake Café baked 340 cupcakes and 40 cakes on Friday. They sold 328 cupcakes and 32 cakes. How many cupcakes were left? (1)

    0-7682-2913-8 *Fast Ideas for Busy Teachers: Math*

How Many Steps Forward? Game Cards

9

The Cupcake Café had a slow day on Tuesday. They baked 323 cupcakes, but sold only 188. If each cupcake cost $2, how much money did they make? (2)

10

A cake big enough for 12 people costs $18 at the Cupcake Café. Cupcakes costs $2 each. Abe is having a party and needs enough food for 11 people. Which would cost Abe more, a cake or 11 cupcakes? (2)

11

Jerry borrowed 4 books from the library on Monday. On Tuesday, he returned 2 and took out 1 more. On Wednesday, he borrowed 4 more. On Friday, he returned the rest of the books. How many books did he return on Friday? (3)

12

Anna, Hannah, and Shelly went apple picking. Anna picked 22 apples, Hannah picked 28, and Shelly picked 24. How many apples did they pick altogether? (1)

13

Andy picked 26 apples, Hank picked 29, and Sherman picked 23. After a while they were hungry so they each ate one of their apples. Then it started to rain. They all ran for shelter, but Andy spilled 3 apples on the way. Hank spilled 7 apples, and Sherman spilled 2 apples. How many apples did the three boys have left when they got to the shelter? (3)

14

Mike bought two dozen balloons. When he put them in his car, three popped. It was a very hot day. On his way home, four more popped from the heat. How many balloons made it home with Mike? (3)

15

Mrs. Kline baked bread. She decided to double the recipe. The recipe called for 5 eggs. How many eggs did Mrs. Kline need? (1)

16

John's Jean Store had a big sale on jeans one weekend. They sold 127 pairs of jeans on Saturday and 143 pairs on Sunday. On Monday, customers returned 21 pairs of jeans. How many jeans did customers keep? (2)

0-7682-2913-8 *Fast Ideas for Busy Teachers: Math*

Making Change for $1, $5, and $10

Updating Alexander

A classic book about subtracting money is *Alexander, Who Used to Be Rich Last Sunday* by Judith Viorst. As you read the book aloud, have your students do the subtraction as Alexander keeps spending his money.

If none of the students comment on the prices in the book, ask them if they think the prices Alexander paid are about right. Explain that the book was written in 1973, and many of the prices seem quite low to us today.

Follow-up by having students write their own updated version of Alexander's story. Ask the class to agree on how much they think Alexander's grandparents would give him now. Have everyone start with that amount. Students can write an abbreviated version of how Alexander spent his money with at least three expenditures that leave him without any money left.

What Were the Coins? Crossword

You could use the crossword activity "What Were the Coins?" as an overhead transparency and complete as a group, assign it for homework, or have students complete it in class.

Thanks for Dining With Us!

Students become cashiers at a restaurant as they complete the activity "Thanks for Dining with Us." Extend this activity by having students create restaurant checks for a group of three or four diners. They can take their restaurant checks and play money in the form of one, five, and/or ten-dollar bills to a "cashier." The cashier determines the amount of change needed and writes it on the back of the check. (No charge cards accepted.) "Customers" double-check the amount of change.

More About Money

Three great books about money for the math book basket or learning center are:

- *Follow the Money* by Loreen Leedy: Students follow the adventures of a quarter from the mint through the bank to a yard sale, then on to a pet store, grocery store, soda machine, and piggy bank.

- *Sluggers' Car Wash* by Stuart J. Murphy: A baseball team sets up a car wash to raise money to buy team shirts, making change for their customers as they go.

- *Money* by Joe Cribb: Part of the Eyewitness series, this book offers fascinating information and images of money from different times and places.

0-7682-2913-8 *Fast Ideas for Busy Teachers: Math*

◆◆ What Were the Coins? ....

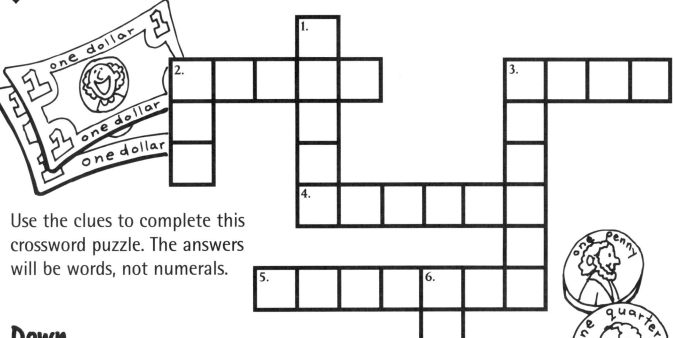

Use the clues to complete this crossword puzzle. The answers will be words, not numerals.

Down

1. Abby's lunch cost $3.30. She gave the cashier $4.00. She got _____ dimes back.

2. Patrick paid for an $8 used video game with a $10 bill. He got _____ dollars back.

3. Katie bought two books for $4.50 each. She gave the cashier $10 and got one _____ back.

6. Jimmie sold his old skateboard at his family's yard sale for $3.50. The girl who bought it gave him a five-dollar bill. Jimmie gave her one dollar and _____ nickels back.

Across

2. Charlie's lunch cost $3.72. He gave the cashier $4.00. He got one quarter and _____ pennies back.

3. The bus cost 45¢. Haley gave the bus driver $1 for herself and her sister. The driver gave Haley a _____ back.

4. Riko bought two books that cost $3.85 each. She gave the cashier $10. She got two dollar bills, a dime, and a _____ back.

5. Ethan paid for a 75¢ ball with a $1 bill. He got one coin back. It was a _____.

© McGraw-Hill Children's Publishing

0-7682-2913-8 *Fast Ideas for Busy Teachers: Math*

Name _____ Date _____

 # Thanks for Dining with Us! ....

The waiters and waitresses bring the cashier these checks and money. Write the amount of change the cashier will make for each one.

BLT   2.95
FRIES   + 1.15
            $4.10

1. Change
_____

OMLET   3.40
HOT DOG   2.45
HAM &
CHEESE   3.20
CHILI   + 1.30
          $10.35
4. Change
_____

CLUB
SANDWICH 3.45
SOUP   2.40
ICED TEA + 1.10
          $6.95
2. Change
_____

BURGER
SODA   2.60
ONION   1.25
RINGS   + 1.45
          $5.30
5. Change
_____

SOUP   2.25
TEA   + .65
          $2.90

3. Change
_____

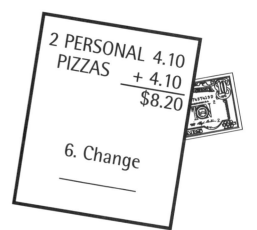

2 PERSONAL 4.10
PIZZAS   + 4.10
          $8.20

6. Change
_____

0-7682-2913-8 *Fast Ideas for Busy Teachers: Math*

Making Change

Flea Market Bargains

Students can practice making change by setting up their own booths in your classroom flea market. To prepare for the sale, have each student cut pictures of six to eight items from old magazines to "sell" at the flea market. Students will need to price each item. Items should be priced between 1¢ and $8.

Give each student a set amount of play money. (Students could also make their own from construction paper.) $15 works well, divided as follows: one $5 bill, eight $1 bills, one half dollar, three quarters, five dimes, two nickels, and fifteen pennies.

When items are priced, students can display them on their desks. Divide the class into thirds. One third can be sellers while the other two groups browse and buy. Each student should make at least one "purchase." Sellers will need to make change for purchases.

After a few minutes, have students change roles, then change again a few minutes later, so everyone gets a chance buying as well as selling. When the flea market closes, discuss what they learned about selling and making change. Discuss problems they had and ideas for solutions.

Coin Display

While learning about money, set up a coin display in the math center featuring quarters from different states, old coins, or coins from different countries. You can use real coins, images from books or the Internet, or a combination of both.

After studying the designs on state quarters, ask students to design their own coins representing the city where they live.

What Shall We Have for Lunch?

Collect menus from several local restaurants—places which have carry-out menus are ideal. (Some places may have menus at their websites or be willing to fax copies to you.) Each student will need a menu. If you don't have menus from enough restaurants, photocopy some so every student can have one.

Select one menu for a demonstration. Ask a student to select items to order from the menu. As the student chooses items, write the prices on the board. Students should write the prices on paper and then add to find the total.

Since lunch is "on you" today, you'll let the class know how much money you're giving the cashier. They can calculate the amount of change you should receive.

After the demonstration, give each student a copy of a menu. Have them write their lunch orders on paper, find the total, and determine the amount of change from a ten- or twenty-dollar bill.

McGraw-Hill Children's Publishing

0-7682-2913-8 *Fast Ideas for Busy Teachers: Math*

Multiplying by 6, 7, and 8

6s, 7s, and 8s Bingo

The six, seven, and eight multiplication facts are often the most difficult for students to master and the ones they to need practice most. Playing "6s, 7s, and 8s Bingo" provides a fun way to practice.

Make a copy of the blank bingo card page for each student. Students fill out the three bingo cards by writing the products of the given number and the numbers 1 through 12. For the 6s bingo card, students write in the numbers 6, 12, 18, 24, etc. Numbers can be written in any order.

24	54	12
72	6	42
36	66	30
48	18	60

Multiplication = Repeated Addition

A 100 number board is a "must-have" for the math center. With a 100 number board, students who are struggling with multiplication can "see" multiplication as a process of repeated addition.

Demonstrate how repeated addition relates to multiplication on a 100 number board. $(2 + 2 + 2$ is the same as $3 \times 2)$.

If students are just beginning to learn their 6, 7, and 8 multiplication facts or need review, lead them as a group by stating the equations ($6 \times 1 = \ldots$, $6 \times 2 = \ldots$ etc.) and having the group answer. Students use the answers to fill in their cards.

Students will need the completed boards and game markers to cover the answers. Prepare slips of paper with the numbers 1 through 12 written on them.

Draw a number and announce it. Students multiply that number times six and cover the product with a game marker. The first one to cover a column of four in a row is the winner. (Rows and diagonals do not count, but you could play four corners as an option.)

Prepare game cards and play the same for the 7s and 8s Bingo games.

 0-7682-2913-8 *Fast Ideas for Busy Teachers: Math*

6s, 7s, and 8s Bingo Cards

6s Bingo

7s Bingo

8s Bingo

McGraw-Hill Children's Publishing

0-7682-2913-8 *Fast Ideas for Busy Teachers: Math*

Multiplying One- and Two-Digit Numbers

Tic x Tac = Toe

Most children enjoy playing Tic-Tac-Toe. With a few simple changes, this game can provide a fun way to practice multiplication.

To play Tic x Tac = Toe, divide the class into pairs. Draw one (or both) of the sample Tic x Tac = Toe layouts on the board. See diagrams below. Have students copy the sample Tic x Tac = Toe board on their papers with the Ss and Ds marked as shown.

Level one:

S	S	S
S	D	S
S	S	S

Level two:

D	S	D
S	D	S
D	S	D

Before a player can mark an X or an O on this Tic-Tac-Toe board, she has to answer correctly a multiplication equation from the other player. If the player wants to mark a spot marked with an S, her partner states a one-digit by one-digit multiplication equation (3 x 6). If the player wants to mark a spot with a D, her partner asks her to solve a one-digit by two-digit equation (2 x 12; 10 x 5).

Students can write the equations and answers on their game sheets. You or one of the better math students can double-check any answers if players are unsure.

Marching to the Picnic Poster

Read Elinor Pinczes's *One Hundred Hungry Ants* aloud to your class as part of a unit on multiplication. To extend students' thinking about the story, have them work together to make a "Getting to the Picnic" poster. They will need five copies of the "Marching to the Picnic" page. Students make arrays showing different ways the ants marched to the picnic.

The poster provides a good visualization of multiplication. The arrays also provide a wonderful way to introduce students to the idea that 50 x 2 is the same as 2 x 50. Regardless of which way you look at the ants, whether it is 2 rows of 50 or 50 rows of 2, it's the same array and the same number of ants arriving at the picnic.

0-7682-2913-8 *Fast Ideas for Busy Teachers: Math*

Marching to the Picnic Pattern ....

0-7682-2913-8 *Fast Ideas for Busy Teachers: Math*

Using Multiplication to Solve Math Stories

What's Your Best Guess?
Using Multiplication to Estimate

Most children enjoy contests involving guessing how many candies, marbles, coins, or other items are in a jar. With Stuart J. Murphy's book *Betcha,* you can link this enthusiasm to multiplication. In *Betcha,* two boys use multiplication to help them estimate in a number of different situations.

As you read the book, stop on page 9 and ask students, "Could multiplication help the boys guess the number of people? How could it help?" Stop on page 15 to ask the questions again.

In conjunction with reading the book, you could set up a guessing station in the math center and have students guess the number of items in several different jars. Let students make a guess before reading and again after reading the book.

> **Math All Around Us**
>
> Many books help students find math in the world around them, like Jon Scieszka's humorous *Math Curse* and Loreen Leedy's clever *2 x 2 = Boo: A Set of Spooky Multiplication Stories.* Both of these books are great resources for students to keep in the math center.

Plate x Plate x Plate = Dirty Dishes

If students look, they can find math at home, at school, at stores, and in sports—from how many forks or dishes a family uses at dinner to points scored in a football game.

The activity "Plate x Plate x Plate = Dirty Dishes" helps students make a connection between math and a common, everyday situation. After they complete this structured activity, challenge them to write at least three "real world" math sentences on their own to share with the class.

Cross Number Challenge

Math stories can be daunting, but putting them in puzzle form can provide a different twist. Students use multiplication to solve word problems with the activity "Cross Number Challenge."

0-7682-2913-8 *Fast Ideas for Busy Teachers: Math*

Name _____ Date _____

 # Plate x Plate x Plate = Dirty Dishes........

Nobody likes doing dishes. Have you ever noticed how they seem to multiply after a big meal? Fill out the chart below after dinner to learn how plates, cups, and silverware can become multiplication equations.

1. How many people ate dinner at your house tonight? _____

2. How many cups or glasses did each person use? _____

   So, _____ people x _____ cups/glasses = _____ dirty cup and glasses.

3. How many plates and bowls did each person use? _____

   Then _____ people x _____ plates and bowls = _____ dirty plates and bowls.

4. How many knives, forks, and spoons did each person use? _____

   That means that _____ people x _____ knives, forks, spoons =

   _____ dirty knives, forks, and spoons.

What other multiplication stories are happening at your house today?

Write three examples.

A. _____

   _____

B. _____

   _____

C. _____

   _____

© McGraw-Hill Children's Publishing

0-7682-2913-8 *Fast Ideas for Busy Teachers: Math*

Cross Number Challenge...........................

Use the clues below to fill in
the numbers in this cross
number puzzle.

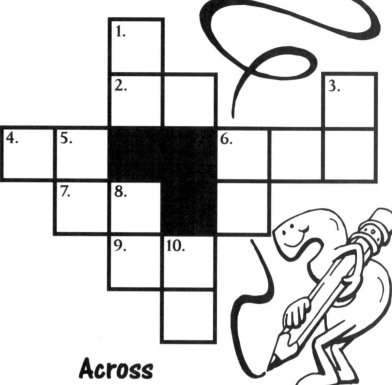

Down

1. One winter Mrs. Lee decided to knit mittens for all her grandchildren. She has 9 grandchildren. How many mittens did she knit?

3. Peter invited 12 friends to his birthday party. His mother bought 5 treats for each guest. How many treats did she buy?

5. Rosie made pancakes for a table of 4 people in her restaurant. Each person ordered 3 pancakes. How many pancakes did Rosie make?

6. Another group of people ordered 5 pancakes each. Rosie made 55 pancakes for the group. How many people were in the group?

8. At the beginning of the school year, Ms. Humes bought 7 packages of paintbrushes for her class. Each package held 6 brushes. How many new brushes did Ms. Humes buy?

10. At the beginning of the year, Ms. Humes also bought 8 sets of tempera paints. Each set had 6 jars of paint. How many jars of tempera paint did Ms. Humes have?

Across

2. At baseball camp there are 8 cabins with 5 boys in each cabin. There are also 8 cabins with 5 girls in each. How many campers are there?

4. Dan, Brian, and Sam are going to camp for a week. Each boy needs one pair of pants for each day of camp. How many pairs of pants should their mother pack for the 3 boys?

6. At baseball camp, 12 campers each hit 10 home runs. How many home runs did those 12 hit?

7. There are 6 hens on Sunnyhill Farm. Each hen laid 4 eggs on Saturday. How many eggs were there altogether?

9. Leena bought 2 dozen eggs at Sunnyhill Farm. How many eggs did she buy?

0-7682-2913-8 *Fast Ideas for Busy Teachers: Math*

Identifying Units and Attributes for Measuring

Take a Page from Measuring Penny

Lisa, the little girl in Loreen Leedy's wonderful book *Measuring Penny*, has an assignment to measure something, and the something she chooses is her dog Penny. Lisa measures Penny's nose and tail. She measures how high Penny can jump, how thirsty she is, and much, much more. As Lisa measures, students learn about measuring in standard and nonstandard units of measure for length, weight, time, volume, and temperature.

After reading this book together, have students choose their own something to measure using the activity page "Measuring _____." Once they have their data, students could make a poster about what they measured, write their own short book modeled on *Measuring Penny*, or give an oral report. Sharing what and how they measured is an important step in learning.

A Measuring Museum

A unit on measuring lends itself perfectly to creating a classroom hands-on measuring museum. Ask each student to bring in several items that relate to measuring. (You might bring in a few spares for students who forget.)

Items could be tools for measuring with various units marked on them (ruler, tape measure, cup) or items with measurements on the label, such as an empty cereal box. Have students make a label for each item that includes their name, the name of the item, what it could be used to measure, and what units it uses.

On "opening day" of the museum, students can display their artifacts on their desks. Let students walk through the museum and examine the artifacts. If you have space in the math center, set up a display for a week or two with one item from each student. If space is a problem, you could take photographs and let students make a poster of your museum.

Ten-Inch Voices, Please

Instead of referring to "inside" and "outside" voices or simply asking students to lower their voices when they are being a bit too loud, consider using terms like "ten-inch voices" and "ten-foot voices." A ten-inch voice would be appropriate when students work quietly in pairs so that only someone ten inches away from the speaker can hear. Ten-foot voices would be appropriate when a student makes a presentation to the whole class. Besides giving you more options than just inside/outside voices, using these terms encourages students to become familiar with different measurement terms and the distances they represent.

 0-7682-2913-8 *Fast Ideas for Busy Teachers: Math*

Name _____ Date _____

◆◆ Measuring _____

Like Lisa in the book *Measuring Penny*, you will measure something in many different ways.

Use standard and nonstandard units.
Make at least one comparison.
Record your results below.

I am going to measure _____

My Measurements
(Each measurement should have a number and a unit.)

I made these measurements using standard units:

1. _____

2. _____

3. _____

I made these measurements using nonstandard units:

1. _____

2. _____

3. _____

Here's a comparison I made:

_____

_____

_____

_____

0-7682-2913-8 *Fast Ideas for Busy Teachers: Math*

Identifying Units and Attributes for Measuring

Measuring Around Town

To fill a few minutes at the end of class, give your students a "Measuring Around Town" challenge question. Select a business or government office such as a grocery store, post office, gas station, bakery, pizza parlor, doctor's office, factory, etc., and ask students to work with a partner or as table groups to brainstorm for ideas about what people in that business or office might need to measure and what units they might use.

To make this a game, award one point for each good answer and an extra point if no other group thought of that answer. You could keep a running tally of points over the course of a week and announce the winners on Friday afternoon.

Measuring Word Sort

Give students the activity "Word Sort" at the beginning of a unit on measurement to see what they already know and to engage them in using their knowledge. This could also be used at the end of the unit as an assessment tool.

If you prefer, students could complete the activity in pairs or small groups. Encourage them to add other measurement words not listed to the appropriate circles.

What Am I?

You can use the activity "What Am I?" to assess how much students have learned toward the end of a unit on measuring or as a review page.

All About Measuring

Many picture books encourage learning about measurement. These are well worth including in the math book basket:

How Tall, How Short, How Far Away by David Adler provides a simple introduction to the history of measurements from Roman times through the creation of the metric system.

Super Sand Castle Saturday by Stuart J. Murphy relates the story of three children and a sand castle-building contest to reinforce the difference between standard and nonstandard units of measurement.

Biggest, Strongest, Fastest by Steve Jenkins offers statistics on the world's biggest, strongest, and fastest creatures. In addition to stating information in standard units, each spread includes a silhouette of the featured animal comparing it to a human figure or some part of a human figure.

0-7682-2913-8 *Fast Ideas for Busy Teachers: Math*

 Word Sort ....

The words in the box are all related to measuring. Sort them out and write them in the circles in groups that belong together. Each circle has one word to get you started.

gallon	year	ounce	pint	foot
meter	inch	mile	millimeter	quart
liter	centimeter	minute	cup	kilometer
hour	ton	day	gram	

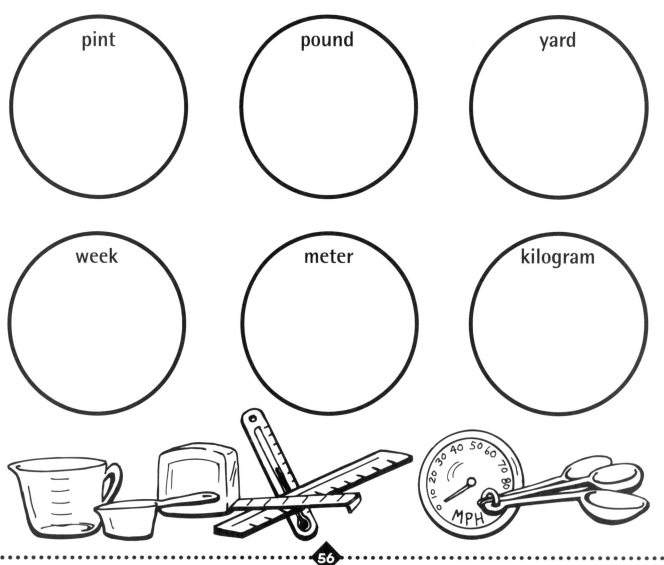

pint

pound

yard

week

meter

kilogram

0-7682-2913-8 *Fast Ideas for Busy Teachers: Math*

 # Identifying and Using Measuring Tools

How Many Third Graders High?

Virtually anything can be used as a nonstandard measuring tool, but it can be especially fun for students to measure items with parts of their bodies or by "pacing off" a given distance.

Get students thinking about nonstandard measurement units by asking questions like:

How many thumbs long is your math book?
What could you measure using "finger paces"?
What could you measure using one of your feet?
Would links or pencils work better as a measuring tool to find the length of your desk?

Let students suggest other nonstandard units and tools they could use to measure.

A fun challenge for the class could be to find how many third graders high your school is. It wouldn't be practical for students to stand on each other's heads, but if you know (or can estimate) the height, cut a piece of string that long. Lay it out on the playground or in a long hallway. Have students lie down along the string to find the answer.

Who's Taller, You or Your Shadow?

Hands-on practice measuring with a ruler, yardstick, tape measure, thermometer, and scale provides a very important skill for students. Practice can be more fun if students get to measure "quirky" things like smiles, frowns, or their shadows at several different times during the day. Let them weigh or measure their sneakers, backpacks, classroom pets, their three favorite books, or the length of a sunbeam. Give them free rein, and they'll come up with lots of things to measure.

For more practice measuring, students can work in pairs to complete the activity, "Me and My Shadow."

Indoor Bocce

Playing bocce makes measuring fun. In this game, one player throws a small ball out onto a lawn. Players then take turns trying to throw their own, larger balls as close to the target ball as possible. If you have an outdoor bocce set, students can play outside at recess, but bocce can be a great indoor, rainy-day game of measurement, too.

To play indoor bocce, students can make small balls from crumpled up aluminum foil. The target ball could a larger ball of foil. After each throw, players measure how close they are to the target ball and keep a record. Each player gets two throws per round. The person who gets closest to the target ball receives one point for the round.

          0-7682-2913-8 *Fast Ideas for Busy Teachers: Math*

Name _____ Date _____

 # Me and My Shadow.................................

Work with a partner. Fill in the blanks. Remember to include the units you used.

Today I measured myself. I am _____ tall.

Measure your shadow at two different times of the day.

At ____:____ my shadow was _____ long.

At ____:____ my shadow was _____ long.

When I stretch my arms out, I am _____ long from fingertip to fingertip.

My smile is _____ wide.

My frown is _____ wide.

My longest toe is _____ long.

My left thumb is _____ long.

My hair is _____ long.

My backpack weighs _____

when it has _____ in it.

My right shoe weighs _____.

   0-7682-2913-8 *Fast Ideas for Busy Teachers: Math*

Name _____ Date _____

 **What Am I?**......

Use the words in the box to answer the riddles.

centimeter	liter	mile	ounce	quart
ruler	scale	tape measure	thermometer	yardstick

1. I would be good for weighing a dog at the vet.

   What am I? _____

2. I measure inches, but I am too long to keep in your desk.

   What am I? _____

3. I measure the temperature.

   What am I? _____

4. You use me to measure length and I do fit in your desk.

   What am I? _____

5. I could help you measure the size of your wrist or the length
   of your room.

   What am I? _____

6. I am a metric unit for measuring milk or soda.

   What am I? _____

7. I am not a metric unit. I measure weight. I am quite small.

   What am I? _____

8. I measure the distance between cities.

   What am I? _____

9. I measure milk or ice cream. I am not a metric unit.

   What am I? _____

10. I measure length. I am smaller than an inch. I am a metric unit.

    What am I? _____

• ◆**59**◆ •

© McGraw-Hill Children's Publishing   0-7682-2913-8 *Fast Ideas for Busy Teachers: Math*

Identifying Symmetry

Do You See Symmetry?

Most students enjoy exploring lines of symmetry. This activity helps them find symmetry in everyday objects. Collect 10 to 20 small items and place them in a shoe box or paper grocery bag. Label the box or bag "Do You See Symmetry?"

Include items that are symmetrical and ones that are not. Items that work well include coins (which have symmetry in their shapes, but not in their designs), leaves, chess game pieces, small boxes, letters of the alphabet cut from newspaper headlines (include capital T, H, M, or O for symmetry), shells, small stones, pressed flowers, plastic dinosaurs, dice, a toothbrush, comb, paper clip, spoon, and fork. Label each object with its name or a number. Include copies of the recording page, "Can I See Symmetry?"

Let students explore the items and complete the recording page when they have free time or as a rainy-day activity. Encourage students to add small items to the symmetry collection.

Symmetry Line-Up

When it's time to line up, ask students, "Who is wearing something symmetrical today?" As students raise their hands, ask them to show or name the item. If it has symmetry, they line up first. Encourage students who can't think of anything symmetrical by asking questions until they realize they do have something symmetrical. (Most items of clothing are symmetrical. Necklaces, patterns on clothing, holes for shoelaces, or pigtails in hair are also possibilities.)

Not-Quite-Right Clowns

The eight clowns on the activity page "Not-Quite-Right Clowns" give students the opportunity to practice looking for symmetry.

Exploring Snowflakes

Snowflakes provide particularly beautiful and intriguing examples of symmetry in the real world. While studying symmetry, you could read *Snowflake Bentley*, Jacqueline Briggs Martin and Mary Azarian's Caldecott-winning biography of snowflake photographer Wilson Bentley.

Students can explore the multiple lines of symmetry in the illustrations and photographs throughout the book. As a follow-up, they can cut out paper snowflakes and decorate them with glue and glitter to make a lovely display of shapes with symmetry.

0-7682-2913-8 *Fast Ideas for Busy Teachers: Math*

Name _____ Date _____

 # Can I See Symmetry? ....

I found symmetry in these objects:	I did not find symmetry in these objects:
_____	_____
_____	_____
_____	_____
_____	_____
_____	_____

Draw two of the objects. Show the lines of symmetry.

0-7682-2913-8 *Fast Ideas for Busy Teachers: Math*

Name _____ Date _____

 # Not Quite Symmetrical Clowns..................

These clowns want to pose for a poster showing symmetry, but none of the clowns is quite ready. Find what is missing on each clown and draw it to make the clown symmetrical.

Color the clowns.

0-7682-2913-8 *Fast Ideas for Busy Teachers: Math*

Representing Probability Outcomes

Quality Control at Ms. Top's Toy Factory

Games and the idea of what is fair are other ways to engage students in an exploration of probability. Talk about games students know well and discuss the difference between games of chance and games of skill. Do the games use dice, a spinner, a game board, or cards? What other items are used in games of chance? Are rolling dice, flipping a coin, or playing scissors-rock-paper fair? Why or why not?

After discussing these questions, students can complete the activity "Quality Control at Ms. Top's Toy Factory."

A Bad Day Makes a Good Start

Children seem to relate well to stories about bad days and Stuart J. Murphy makes good use of that fact in his entertaining introduction to probability, *Probably Pistachio*. Reading and discussing this book as a group can be a great introduction to a unit on probability. Take time to stop and discuss Jack's problems and his predictions, as well as the use of words and phrases like **probably, usually, always,** and **an even chance** as you read.

Is it Fair?

Set up a probability station in the math center to provide an opportunity for students to explore probability. They will need a coin, a paper bag with two blue game chips and three red game chips, and copies of the activity page "Is It Fair?"

After students have completed the activity, discuss their findings.

Certainly, Probably, Possibly, Unlikely, Never

Making predictions can be fun, especially when approached with a sense of humor. Making a class poster of predictions in five categories helps students explore these important words and the probability concepts behind them.

You could start this activity by reading *Cloudy with a Chance of Meatballs* by Judi Barrett, which invites readers to think about absolutely absurd predictions that could never really happen.

Prepare a large sheet of paper or poster board by writing the category titles *Certainly, Probably, Possibly, Unlikely,* and *Never* in marker. Students can work in small groups to brainstorm for ideas and make lists of their own predictions in all five categories. Have each group select two ideas from each category that they like best. A representative from each group can write the group's best ideas on the poster. Display the poster as a fun reminder of what these terms mean.

 0-7682-2913-8 *Fast Ideas for Busy Teachers: Math*

Name _____ Date _____

 # Is It Fair? Find Out for Yourself...............

Select one of the experiments. Number a sheet of lined paper from 1 to 100 to record the results of your experiment.

Activity #1: Coin Toss

1. Flip a coin.

2. Did it land on heads or tails? Record your result by writing H or T on the first line.

3. Flip the coin 99 more times and record your results after each toss.

4. How many times did it land on heads? _____

5. How many times did it land on tails? _____

6. Is flipping a coin fair? _____

   Why or why not? _____

   _____

Activity #2: What's More Likely, Red or Blue?
Before you start, check that there are three red game chips and two blue game chips in the bag.

1. Without looking, draw one game chip from the bag.

2. Is it red or blue? Record your result by writing R or B on the first line.

3. Return the game chip to the bag. Shake the bag and draw again. Do this 99 more times and record the results each time.

4. How many times did you choose a red game chip? _____

5. How many times did you choose a blue game chip? _____

6. Is it fair? _____

   Why or why not? _____

   _____

0-7682-2913-8 *Fast Ideas for Busy Teachers: Math*

Name _____ Date _____

 # Quality Control at Ms. Top's Toy Factory

Congratulations! You've been hired by Ms. Top to check her new designs for spinners. Your job is to make sure the spinners are fair.

If a spinner is fair, circle the word "fair."
If it is not fair, circle the word "unfair" and tell why.

1. fair   unfair

   Reason: _____

   _____

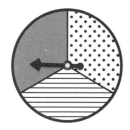

2. fair   unfair

   Reason: _____

   _____

3. fair   unfair

   Reason: _____

   _____

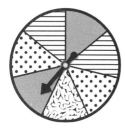

4. fair   unfair

   Reason: _____

   _____

       0-7682-2913-8 *Fast Ideas for Busy Teachers: Math*

Representing Probability Outcomes ....

How's the Weather?

Weather forecasts provide a very accessible way to relate probability to an everyday, familiar situation. Talk about the weather forecast for the following day sometime toward the end of your school day. If you have access to the Internet, a student can easily check the next day's prediction for precipitation for your area. Link percentages to probability terms by having students select one term and write it by each day's forecast. Use the terms **certainly, probably, possibly, probably not**, and **definitely not**.

As a group, create and fill in a five-day class chart like the sample shown below. Based on the prediction, the group should choose and circle one of the probability terms.

The forecast for Tuesday is for a _____% chance of _____.		
The best term to describe the forecast would be: _____		
Was the forecast correct?	Yes	No
The forecast for Wednesday is for a _____% chance of _____.		
The best term to describe the forecast would be: _____		
Was the forecast correct?	Yes	No
The forecast for Thursday is for a _____% chance of _____.		
The best term to describe the forecast would be: _____		
Was the forecast correct?	Yes	No
The forecast for Friday is a for _____% chance of _____.		
The best term to describe the forecast would be: _____		
Was the forecast correct?	Yes	No
The forecast for Saturday is for a _____% chance of _____.		
The best term to describe the forecast would be: _____		
Was the forecast correct?	Yes	No

0-7682-2913-8 *Fast Ideas for Busy Teachers: Math*

Computing Elapsed Time

How Do You Spend Your Day?

A great way to begin a unit on computing elapsed time is to have students complete the activity "How Do You Spend Your Day?" Collect their activity pages and use the information to create personal, real-life math stories for the class to solve, such as, "Josh woke up at 7:00 a.m. on Monday. He left for school at 8:15. How long after he woke up did Josh leave for school?"

Extension:

After learning about computing elapsed time, you could return the activity pages to students and have them calculate the amount of time they spent on each activity. They could write the answers in a column on the right side of the page.

How Long Did You Sleep?

Have students select the elapsed time for one of the items from the activity page "How Do You Spend Your Day?" like the amount of time they slept or watched TV. Using a calculator, have them calculate the amount of time they would spend doing that activity for one week, one month, and one year. Some of the answers will probably surprise your students!

Countdown to Lunch

Another simple way to practice computing elapsed time with the class is to have a daily countdown. You could countdown the time until lunch, afternoon recess, math class, or any other event.

At the beginning of the day, write on the board:

Time We Have Been at School: 0 hours/0 minutes
Time until lunch: 3 hours/0 minutes

The first day, change the numbers for both categories at various times during the day. On following days, list different events and ask student volunteers to change the countdown clock. Let students suggest what event they will count down to each day.

Elapsed Time Math Stories

Gather a supply of calendars, bus or train schedules, and local or pro sports' team schedules for the math center in a large envelope. (Businesses might be willing to donate outdated ones.) Calendars and schedules do not have to be current for this purpose.

Have students go to the math center and use a calendar page or schedule to write elapsed time math stories for each other to solve.

Examples:

If Joy gets on a bus at Main and Second at 8:15, what time will she arrive at the corner of Avocado Avenue and Banana Boulevard?

Today is May 3. Brad's birthday is on May 19th. How many days until Brad's birthday?

 0-7682-2913-8 *Fast Ideas for Busy Teachers: Math*

Computing Elapsed Time

 # How Do You Spend Your Day?..................

I woke up at _____:_____ (AM   PM).

I was ready to go to school at _____:_____ (AM   PM).

I left for school at _____:_____ (AM   PM).

I got to school at _____:_____ (AM   PM).

I left school at _____:_____ (AM   PM).

After school I read from _____:_____ to _____:_____ (AM   PM).

I watched TV from _____:_____ to _____:_____ (AM   PM).

After school I played from_____:_____ to _____:_____ (AM   PM).

We started dinner at _____:_____ (AM   PM).

We finished dinner at _____:_____ (AM   PM).

I went to bed at _____:_____ (AM   PM).

I woke up the next morning at _____:_____ (AM   PM).

0-7682-2913-8 *Fast Ideas for Busy Teachers: Math*

Computing Elapsed Time

Class Records Poster

Students can practice computing elapsed time as they work together to create a Class Records poster. Make a list of individual and class events that students could time and record on another sheet of paper over a period of a week or two. After gathering data, students record best times on the Class Records poster.

Besides obvious events like playground activities that are usually best timed with a stopwatch, add some silly challenges like saying the alphabet backwards or removing their shoes and putting them back on the wrong feet. Also consider including other events you'd like the class to work on, such as the time it takes for the whole class to complete the math warm-up or the time it takes to line up for lunch and walk quietly to the cafeteria.

Keeping track of records allows you to highlight accomplishments you'd like the class or individuals to work towards. It also provides repeated opportunities for calculating elapsed time, since students will be sure to want to break records.

How Long Have You Been Awake?

Another fun way to link computing time directly to your students' lives is to have them calculate how long they have been awake. When they arrive one morning, ask them to write down what time they woke up today. Several times throughout the day stop and ask them to recalculate how long they have been awake.

That's Impossible!

To interject fun in your unit on computing elapsed time and get students thinking about whether answers to problems about time make sense, give them the activity "That's Impossible!" Ask them to circle and correct the mistakes in calculations in the article.

As a class, make up a "fantastic" group story about an impossible event in which students are the main characters.

Broken Clocks Work Well

To compute elapsed time correctly, skip counting by 5s is an essential skill. Students also need to be able to tell time correctly. If you have an old wristwatch or wind-up alarm clock that doesn't work anymore, add it to the math center. Students use those or any other clock with adjustable hands to work in pairs to practice telling time. Have students take turns making a silly time statement such as, "I ate jelly bean cereal for breakfast at 7:15 today." or "Tomorrow I leave for Mars at 4:30." The other student sets the hands of the clock to that time.

© McGraw-Hill Children's Publishing

0-7682-2913-8 *Fast Ideas for Busy Teachers: Math*

Name _____ Date _____

 # That's Impossible! ....

Read the newspaper story below. Find five mistakes in the time calculations in the story. Circle the mistakes and write the correct amounts of time.

Speedy Third Graders Set New Records

Mt. Everest, Nepal—Two third-graders visiting Nepal from Alaska amazed the world today when they set two new world records.

At 9:20 this morning, Marsha Mountaineer and Marvin Speedyreader woke up and decided to climb Mount Everest. By 10:00 they had gotten dressed, eaten breakfast, and were ready to go in only a half an hour.

They climbed for two hours from 10:00 to 12:30 before stopping for lunch. Lunch took just 10 minutes. After a short rest, they started climbing again.

At 3:00 the two climbers took a break. "I like to read every afternoon around 3:00," said Marvin Speedyreader. Marvin read for 20 minutes from 3:00 to 3:30. He read an entire 800-page book, setting a new record for speed-reading.

They started climbing again at 3:30. They reached the top of the mountain three hours later at 6:00.

"That was fast," said Marsha Mountaineer. "We are the first to ever climb Mount Everest in only three hours!"

Do you think this story is true? Why or why not? _____

_____

0-7682-2913-8 *Fast Ideas for Busy Teachers: Math*

 # Finding Equivalent Fractions

Fraction Fun

Get students thinking about fractions and ways to compare them by reading David Adler's *Fraction Fun*. Adler introduces basic fraction vocabulary, including numerator and denominator, and gives examples of ways we use fractions, like when we slice up a pizza. After reading *Fraction Fun*, give students the activity "Who Ate More Pizza?"

Encourage students to make up similar math stories of their own using fractions with pizza, cake, or other food items they like.

$$\frac{6}{12} = \frac{1}{2}$$

While working with fractions, include empty egg cartons, trays from boxes of candy, or plastic six-pack soda rings in the math learning center. These familiar items can help students to conceptualize fractions and equivalencies.

Students struggling to understand the fraction $\frac{5}{12}$ can use game chips and an egg carton. One game chip in one compartment = $\frac{1}{12}$. To see what $\frac{5}{12}$ looks like, put one game chip in each of five different compartments.

To show equivalent fractions, put one game chip in each of six different compartments and talk about how the chips represent $\frac{6}{12}$. Then cut the egg carton in half to show that $\frac{6}{12}$ is the same as $\frac{1}{2}$ of the whole cartoon.

Three in a Row

Once students have practiced finding equivalent fractions with visual guides and learned how to reduce fractions, they'll be ready to try solving the number puzzle "Three in a Row."

Equivalent Coin Challenges

Coins help students think through and understand the idea of equivalent fractions because the concept of exchanging one set of coins for one another is familiar to them. Use coins to make posters for the math center by gluing real or play coins to poster board and show their fractional value (quarter = $\frac{1}{4}$; dime = $\frac{1}{10}$; nickel = $\frac{1}{20}$; and penny = $\frac{1}{100}$).

Prepare a set of index cards with equivalency math stories for students to solve. Example: If I have $\frac{2}{4}$ of a dollar, how many tenths of a dollar do I have? Also include a set of play coins for students to use as manipulatives to find the answers.

Provide blank index cards and encourage students to write their own math stories to contribute to the center.

  0-7682-2913-8 *Fast Ideas for Busy Teachers: Math*

Comparing Fractions

The Larger Fraction Wins

Divide students into pairs. Give each pair four regular six-sided dice and a fraction comparison chart. Each student shakes two dice and writes a fraction using the numbers shaken by writing the smaller number over the larger one. If a student shakes a two and a three, she writes $\frac{2}{3}$.

If a student shakes a pair, he should shake one die again until he has two different numbers.

Partners compare their fractions using a fraction comparison chart. The one with the larger fraction scores one point. Have students play 10 rounds. The one with the most points wins.

Variations:

Play using a pair of fraction dice.

Have students compare their fractions without using a comparison chart.

Fraction Action

Add these titles to the math book basket while working on fractions.

Fraction Action
by Loreen Leedy

Eating Fractions
by Bruce McMillan

Give Me Half and a Fair Bear Share
by Stuart J. Murphy

The books by Loreen Leedy and Stuart J. Murphy include fraction activities to use in the classroom.

Fraction Masters

Divide students into teams. Challenge each team to find several ways to express a given fraction. If you say one-half, they could write $\frac{2}{4}$, $\frac{3}{6}$, $\frac{4}{8}$, $\frac{5}{10}$, etc. The teams write as many equivalent fractions as possible in a given amount of time.

Vary the difficulty level in the fractions you name and the time you allow teams to write their answers. After each fraction, review their answers. Award 1 point for each correct answer. Award 2 points for a correct answer not written by any other team. Write the score for each team on the board. Play several rounds to see which team can be the Fraction Masters of the day.

See Through Fractions

Overhead transparency sheets help students see how fractions compare. In advance, draw five identical shapes (circles, rectangles, squares) on separate transparency sheets. Divide one shape in half, one into thirds, one into quarters, one into fifths, and one into sixths. Use these to pose a series of true or false questions (Is $\frac{1}{2}$ larger than $\frac{3}{4}$?). Explore the answers by coloring in the transparencies and putting one on top of the other. Is $\frac{1}{2}$ larger than $\frac{3}{4}$? The answer will be very clear when you place one top of the other.

0-7682-2913-8 *Fast Ideas for Busy Teachers: Math*

Name _____ Date _____

 # Who Ate More Pizza?..

Elias and Ellen are twins. They both love pizza, and they both try to eat the most pizza at dinner. One week their parents agreed they could eat pizza every single night.

Color in the fractions of pizza each one ate every day. Then answer the question, "Who ate more pizza?"

Monday

Elias ate $\frac{1}{4}$ of a pizza.

Ellen ate $\frac{3}{8}$ of a pizza.

1. Who ate more pizza? _____

Tuesday

Elias ate $\frac{3}{6}$ of a pizza.

Ellen ate $\frac{3}{8}$ of a pizza.

2. Who ate more pizza? _____

Wednesday

Elias ate $\frac{3}{4}$ of a pizza.

Ellen ate $\frac{11}{12}$ of a pizza.

3. Who ate more pizza? _____

Thursday

Elias ate $\frac{4}{6}$ of a pizza.

Ellen ate $\frac{1}{2}$ a pizza.

4. Who ate more pizza? _____

Friday

Elias didn't feel well, so he ate only $\frac{1}{8}$ of a pizza.

Ellen wasn't too hungry, either. She only ate $\frac{1}{10}$ of a pizza.

5. Who ate more pizza? _____

0-7682-2913-8 *Fast Ideas for Busy Teachers: Math*

 **Three in a Row**...

Look backwards, forwards, up, down, and diagonally to find three fractions in a row with the same value. Circle the equivalent fractions.

$\frac{8}{12}$	$\frac{4}{6}$	$\frac{2}{3}$	$\frac{2}{6}$	$\frac{7}{8}$	$\frac{6}{8}$
$\frac{2}{10}$	$\frac{1}{2}$	$\frac{1}{4}$	$\frac{2}{8}$	$\frac{3}{12}$	$\frac{3}{4}$
$\frac{1}{5}$	$\frac{6}{8}$	$\frac{2}{4}$	$\frac{3}{9}$	$\frac{4}{4}$	$\frac{9}{12}$
$\frac{3}{15}$	$\frac{2}{10}$	$\frac{4}{12}$	$\frac{4}{8}$	$\frac{5}{10}$	$\frac{3}{6}$
$\frac{2}{6}$	$\frac{1}{3}$	$\frac{4}{12}$	$\frac{1}{7}$	$\frac{2}{14}$	$\frac{3}{21}$

0-7682-2913-8 *Fast Ideas for Busy Teachers: Math*

◆◆ Dividing with a ◆◆ Single-Digit Divisor

Sharing with Friends

The idea of sharing connects well with division, as Pat Hutchins shows in her wonderful book *The Doorbell Rang*. Reading *The Doorbell Rang* aloud can be a great introduction to a unit on division. Follow up with an activity where students determine how they could share a food treat with several friends.

One approach would be to follow the structure of Hutchins' book. Show two students a plate with 30 cookies. Ask, "If the two of you shared these cookies evenly, how many would you each get?"

Write the division equation on the board, then "remember" two, three, or four more students who should be included. Rewrite the equation and help students find the new answer. Continue "remembering" more students who would want to share the cookies, writing new equations and helping students find the answers, until all students are included. Then the two helpers could divide the cookies among classmates to share.

Another approach would be to give each student a paper cup full of popcorn, small colored candies, or animal crackers. Ask students to count their treats and decide how many each person would get if they shared their treats with one, two, three, four, or five friends.

Make More Mixed-Up Division Puzzles

Make extra copies of the "Create Your Own Mixed-Up Math Puzzle" template for the math center. When students have free time, challenge them to create their own Mixed-Up Division Puzzles using the template. This provides practice creating and solving equations. Have students check their answers using multiplication.

When they finish their puzzles, they can cut them apart and trade with a partner to solve.

Mixed-Up Division Puzzle

Students can complete the activity "Mixed-Up Division Puzzle" to practice basic division facts. Cut the puzzle apart and give each student an envelope with the puzzle pieces. (Save one uncut copy for the Answer Key.) Students can work alone or in pairs to complete the puzzles.

Create your own Mixed-Up Division Puzzles for students to practice other division facts using the template "Create Your Own Mixed-Up Math Puzzle" on page 11. To create a new puzzle, write the equations by the question marks and the corresponding answers in the blanks indicated by the arrows.

© McGraw-Hill Children's Publishing   0-7682-2913-8 *Fast Ideas for Busy Teachers: Math*

Mixed-Up Division Puzzle

$5\overline{)45}$	9 $3\overline{)15}$	5 $3\overline{)9}$	3
10 ÷ 2	12 ÷ 2	12 ÷ 6	3 ÷ 3
5 $4\overline{)16}$	6 4 $9\overline{)54}$	2 6 $9\overline{)63}$	1 7
20 ÷ 5	24 ÷ 6	24 ÷ 4	21 ÷ 3
4 $8\overline{)16}$	4 2 $4\overline{)12}$	6 3 $5\overline{)35}$	7 7
48 ÷ 12	32 ÷ 8	27 ÷ 3	55 ÷ 5
4 $2\overline{)22}$	4 11 $6\overline{)54}$	9 9 $5\overline{)25}$	11 5

0-7682-2913-8 *Fast Ideas for Busy Teachers: Math*

 # Dividing with a Remainder

Batter Up!

To build enthusiasm for dividing with remainders, students can compete in a baseball-type game.

Divide students into groups of two to four players. Give each group a copy of the "Batter Up!" game board, 20 index cards, and a six-sided game cube. Each student will need a game marker, pencil, and paper.

To play, students write a two-digit number on each index card and place the cards facedown in pile. The first player draws a number card and shakes the game cube, then divides the number on the card by the number on the game cube. The remainder, if any, determines how many bases he advances. If the remainder is one, he moves his game marker to first base. A remainder of five allows a player to move his game marker completely around the bases, scoring a home run and stopping on first base. On his next turn, he continues on from first base.

Players take turns as above, playing nine "innings" in all. More than one player can be on the same base at the same time. Each player uses tally marks to record his or her "home runs." Shuffle and reuse cards as needed. The player with the most home runs wins the game.

How Many Left?

Place 20 to 40 small objects, such as marbles, links, paper clips, etc., in a zipper plastic bag. Make up several bags with different nonfood items in each bag for the math center. Students can count the number of items in each bag, divide them into groups with an even number in each group, and create their own division stories using that number of items.

Example: Tonya had 24 paper clips. She divided the paper clips among six classmates. How many paper clips did each student receive?

Marching Orders

Pat Hutchins introduces division through sharing. Elinor Pinczes takes a different approach, using the idea of being left out to explain division remainders. Introduce the concept of remainders in division by reading *A Remainder of One,* about one poor little bug who keeps getting left out when his regiment marches in a parade. He is the remainder of one.

To explore the concept of remainders further with your class, divide them into pairs or small groups. Give each group a squadron number (16, 24, 30, etc., as in the book). In the 16th squadron there would be 16 bugs, 24 in the 24th squadron, and so on.

Have students find out what would happen if that number of bugs marched in rows of 2s, 3s, 4s, or 5s. How many rows of bugs would there be? Would there be any remainders?

© McGraw-Hill Children's Publishing

0-7682-2913-8 *Fast Ideas for Busy Teachers: Math*

 # Batter Up! Game Board ....

Score Board: Record 1 tally mark for each home run.

Player's Name	Player's Name	Player's Name	Player's Name

2nd Base

3rd Base

1st Base

Home Plate

78

0-7682-2913-8 *Fast Ideas for Busy Teachers: Math*

 **Answer Key** ....

Mr. Top's Trophy Shop, page 13

Mr. Top's new prices should be: Engraving $1; Assorted Ribbons 3 for $1; Regular Rabbit Trophy $6; Best in Show Rabbit Trophy $11; Best in Show Dog Trophy $12; Regular Dog Trophy $6; Swimming Trophy $7; Basketball MVP Award $12; Soccer Cup $28; Soccer MVP Award $12

Sam's Ice Cream Shop, page 14

Sam's new prices should be: Milk Shakes: Small: $1.80; Medium: $2.80; Large: $3.70

Sundaes: Small: $2.00; Medium: $2.90; Large: $4.10

Cones: Single Dip: $1.10; Double Dip: $2.10; Triple Dip: $3.00

Extras: Nuts: 30¢; Whipped Cream: 40¢; Sprinkles: 30¢

A-Mazing Fours, page 16

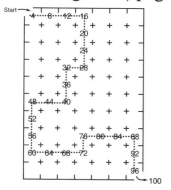

Skip Counting Sequence Search, page 18

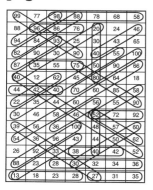

What's Missing? A Cross Number Puzzle, page 25

Check the Checks, pages 27–28

#101: Reject   #102: Accept

#103: Reject   #104: Reject

#105: Accept

Hidden Numbers, page 29

```
9 6 (7 8 0 2 4) 5 9
(1) 3 4 6 (8) 1 3 3 (5)
0  4 0 (1 8 0 1 2) 0
0 (2) 9 1 6 8 9 1 7
4  2 0 2 0 5 3 5 2
2  6 4 (6 (1) 0 7 (2) 1
4 (1 4 2 0 2) 0 2 6
(1 (7) 9 2 0) 4 0 0 2
8  1 6 (4 5 0 0 (1) 3
```

How Many Steps Forward?, pages 39–40

1. 388	9. $376
2. 478	10. 11 cupcakes
3. 253	11. 7
4. 241	12. 74
5. 138	13. 63
6. 5	14. 17
7. 59	15. 10
8. 12	16. 249

© McGraw-Hill Children's Publishing   0-7682-2913-8 *Fast Ideas for Busy Teachers: Math*

Answer Key

What Were the Coins?, page 43

Down

1. seven
2. two
3. dollar
6. ten

Across

2. three
3. dime
4. nickel
5. quarter

Thanks for Dining with Us!, page 44

1. 90¢
2. $3.05
3. 10¢
4. 65¢
5. 70¢
6. $1.80

Cross Number Challenge, page 52

Down

1. 18
3. 60
5. 12
6. 11
8. 42
10. 48

Across

2. 80
4. 21
6. 120
7. 24
9. 24

Word Sort, page 56

Pint: gallon, quart, cup

Pound: ton, ounce

Yard: inch, mile, foot

Week: day, hour, year, minute

Meter: centimeter, millimeter

Kilogram: gram, liter

What Am I?, page 59

1. scale
2. yardstick
3. thermometer
4. ruler
5. tape measure
6. liter
7. ounce
8. mile
9. quart
10. centimeter

Quality Control at Ms. Top's Toy Factory, page 65

Spinner 1: Unfair—60% of spinner is light; 40% is dark;

Spinner 2: Fair—1/3 of spinner is striped; 1/3 is solid; 1/3 has polka-dots

Spinner 3: Unfair—1/5 of spinner is striped; 2/5 is solid; 1/5 has polka-dots; 1/5 has lines

Spinner 4: Unfair—2/7 is striped; 2/7 is solid; 2/7 has polka dots; 1/7 has lines

That's Impossible!, page 70

Mistakes: Paragraph 2: half an hour after 9:20 would be 9:50 not 10:00.

Paragraph 3: They climbed for two and a half hours, not two hours.

Paragraph 4: Marvin read for 30 minutes not 20.

Paragraph 5: 6:00 is two and a half hours after 3:30, not three hours.

Paragraph 6: They climbed for much more than three hours! (Exactly how long is hard to say given the other mistakes.)

Who Ate More Pizza?, page 73

Monday: Ellen

Tuesday: Elias

Wednesday: Ellen

Thursday: Elias

Friday: Elias

Three in a Row, page 74

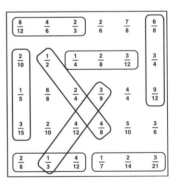

© McGraw-Hill Children's Publishing

0-7682-2913-8 *Fast Ideas for Busy Teachers: Math*